American Prose and Poetry in the 20th Century

Caroline Zilboorg

Series Editor: Adrian Barlow

CAMBRIDGE
UNIVERSITY PRESS

PUBLISHED BY THE PRESS SYNDICATE OF THE UNIVERSITY OF CAMBRIDGE
The Pitt Building, Trumpington Street, Cambridge, United Kingdom

CAMBRIDGE UNIVERSITY PRESS
The Edinburgh Building, Cambridge CB2 2RU, UK
40 West 20th Street, New York, NY 10011–4211, USA
477 Williamstown Road, Port Melbourne, VIC 3207, Australia
Ruiz de Alarcón 13, 28014 Madrid, Spain
Dock House, The Waterfront, Cape Town 8001, South Africa

http://www.cambridge.org

First published 2000
Third printing 2002

Printed in the United Kingdom at the University Press, Cambridge

Typefaces: Clearface and Mixage *System:* QuarkXPress® 4.04

A catalogue record for this book is available from the British Library

ISBN 0 521 663903 paperback

Prepared for publication by Gill Stacey
Designed by Tattersall Hammarling & Silk
Cover photo: Simon Harris, The Robert Harding Picture Library (detail)

Contents

20th century America: key events

1903	Words of Emma Lazarus inscribed on the Statue of Liberty
1914–1918	First World War
1917	U.S. enters First World War; The Russian Revolution
1919	Prohibition
1920	Women get the vote
1929	U.S. stock market crash; first sound movie
1933	Hitler comes to power in Germany; Prohibition repealed
1936–1937	The Spanish Civil War
1939–1945	Second World War
1941	Japanese bomb Pearl Harbor; U.S. enters Second World War
1945	Atomic bombs dropped over Hiroshima and Nagasaki
1950	McCarthy proclaims his list of known communists
1950–1953	Korean War
1953	Julius and Ethel Rosenberg electrocuted
1954	U.S. Supreme court rules that racial segregation is illegal; McCarthy hearings televised
1962	The Cuban missile crisis; Marilyn Monroe dies
1963	John F. Kennedy assassinated
1965	First American combat troops sent to Vietnam
1967	Mass anti-war march against the Pentagon in Washington, D.C.
1968	Martin Luther King and Robert F. Kennedy killed
1969	Stonewall (gay rights) rebellion in New York City; Nixon announces troop withdrawals from Southeast Asia
1970	Four students killed during anti-war demonstration at Kent State University
1973	American troops withdrawn from Vietnam; abortion legalised
1974	Richard Nixon resigns as President
1975	American military involvement in the war in Southeast Asia officially ends
1981	AIDS identified in the U.S.
1999	Impeachment proceedings against Bill Clinton

Presidents

1897–1901	William McKinley
1901–1909	Theodore Roosevelt
1909–1913	William Taft
1913–1921	Woodrow Wilson
1921–1923	Warren G. Harding
1923–1929	Calvin Coolidge
1929–1933	Herbert Hoover
1933–1945	Franklin D. Roosevelt
1945–1953	Harry S. Truman
1953–1961	Dwight D. Eisenhower
1961–1963	John F. Kennedy
1963–1969	Lyndon Johnson
1969–1974	Richard Nixon
1974–1977	Gerald Ford
1977–1981	Jimmy Carter
1981–1989	Ronald Reagan
1989–1993	George Bush
1993–2001	Bill Clinton

Introduction

The literature written by Americans during the 20th century encompasses a wide variety of voices: male and female, rich and poor, urban and rural, white and black and brown and yellow. Their work includes brief lyric poems and epic verse as well as essays, plays, short stories, novellas and novels which attempt to squeeze between their covers the breadth and diversity of American experience. From Maine to Florida, from New York to California, 20th century American writers have struggled to express what it has meant to be simultaneously an individual and part of a nation, a product both of their own time and of history. They have put their feelings and ideas into words and forms that are sometimes conventional and at other times experimental, while they have used their subjects and themes and diction to confront modern experience from a distinctly American perspective.

The significance of context

20th century American literature thus reflects the period in complex ways. To begin with, a century is a large unit of time and needs to be understood as more than the mathematical hundred years used to measure it. T.S. Eliot (1888–1965) suggests in 'Tradition and the Individual Talent', an important essay written in 1919, that no writer 'has his complete meaning alone'. In fact, Eliot explains, the writer must develop 'a perception, not only of the pastness of the past, but of its presence'. This vital sense of history 'compels a man to write not merely with his own generation in his bones, but with a feeling that the whole of the literature of Europe from Homer and within it the whole of the literature of his own country has a simultaneous existence'. Such an historical and geographical awareness involves 'a sense of the timeless as well as of the temporal and of the timeless and the temporal together'; it makes a writer both part of *the tradition* and at the same time 'acutely conscious of his place in time, of his own contemporaneity'. Reading with an awareness of our own period and values, we can begin to understand Eliot's point by noticing his use of masculine pronouns. Like most authors of his own time and throughout history, Eliot thought of the serious writer as a man, while we know that writers can be and probably always have been both men and women. Our 'historical sense', our awareness of our own context as well as the author's, allows us to recognise the significance and usefulness of Eliot's ideas while simultaneously including women in our understanding.

Extending Eliot's ideas, the poet Adrienne Rich (b. 1929) also comments on the importance of history and, for her, the special significance of female experience and geography. Reflecting in 1984 on what it means to be an American writer, she insisted:

> As a woman I have a country; as a woman I cannot divest myself of that country merely by condemning its government or by saying three times 'As a woman my country is the whole world.' Tribal loyalties aside, and even if nation-states are now just pretexts used by multinational conglomerates to serve their interests, I need to understand how a place on the map is also a place in history within which as a woman, a Jew, a lesbian, a feminist I am created and trying to create.

For American writers throughout the 20th century, context is a rich and vital issue; as Eliot and Rich suggest, they confront it not only as history but as geography, not only as national but as individual experience. As the novelist William Faulkner (1897–1962) put it, cryptically but quite eloquently, 'There is no was, only is.'

20th century American history

Another way of understanding the importance of context for our reading of 20th century American literature is to consider the history of the period which stretches from the invention of the automobile early in the century to the invention of computers that now seem, like petrol-powered vehicles, essential to our daily lives. While at the time of the American Civil War (1861–1865), most Americans lived on farms east of the Mississippi River, by the beginning of the First World War, the United States was a world power whose boundaries spanned a continent. When we think of the history of America in the 20th century, we must certainly think of the First World War and the years that followed, the 'Roaring Twenties', the Great Depression, the Japanese bombing of Pearl Harbor, which brought America into the Second World War, and the dropping of atomic bombs on Nagasaki and Hiroshima. We may also think of the economic boom years of the 1950s, the Cold War, the assassinations of John F. Kennedy and Martin Luther King, the civil rights movement and the protests by young people and others throughout the country against America's involvement in Vietnam. We may think of sixties 'hippies' and their experimentation with drugs and 'alternative lifestyles', the 'women's liberation' movement, Richard Nixon's resignation and the AIDS epidemic. Directly or indirectly, American writers experienced these events, and the period's history and atmosphere, values and issues helped to shape the works they wrote.

How this book is organised

Part 1: Reading 20th century American literature

Part 1 looks at events which shaped the lives of individual authors and explores the ideas which directly and indirectly affected what they wrote about and the ways they expressed their thoughts and feelings.

Part 2: Approaching the texts

Part 2 examines the challenge of thinking and writing about 20th century American literature within a variety of specific contexts.

Part 3: Texts and extracts

Part 3 offers a diverse selection of American writing. These prose passages, sections from longer poems and complete short poems illustrate the variety of literary expression in the United States. They also provide additional examples of writing rooted in the contexts described in Part 1.

Part 4: How to write about 20th century American literature

Part 4 considers the task of writing about American literature as well as a range of critical responses.

Part 5: Resources

This part contains a chronology of historical and literary events. It provides suggestions for further reading and advice on using information technology. It also includes a glossary of critical terms. (Terms which appear in the glossary are highlighted in bold type when they first appear in the main text.)

At different points throughout the book, and at the end of Parts 1, 2 and 4, there are tasks and assignments which suggest a variety of contexts through which you might approach an understanding of particular works. The more appropriate or interesting contexts, however, are likely to be those you choose and research yourself.

1 Reading 20th century American literature

Part 1 of *American Prose and Poetry in the 20th Century* begins by looking at modern literature's roots in Colonial America. It then examines the issues and challenges in the 19th century which influenced later writing. It goes on to look in detail at the cultural background which shaped the literature of the First World War, the 'Roaring Twenties', the Great Depression, the Second World War, the post-war period, and the 1960s. Part 1 concludes by examining the diversity of literary response at the end of the millennium.

The historical and social background

- What are the roots of 20th century American literature?
- What ideas, traditions and history did the century's writers respond to?

American writing in the 20th century has its roots in earlier American experience and in the literary expression of the preceding centuries. What it means to write and the subjects, themes and even the language an author uses are rooted in earlier attitudes, values and ways of thinking and being. Sometimes this process seems quite conscious. For example, when Paul Auster (b. 1947) entitles his fifth novel *Leviathan* (1992), he encourages us to read his book in the context of Herman Melville's *Moby Dick* (1851), as well as suggesting that we keep in mind Thomas Hobbes' economic treatise, *Leviathan* (1651), and Jonah's experience inside the biblical whale. Often this contextual process is less explicit, however, and as Eliot suggests, an author writes with history in his or her bones.

Puritan America

One of the important ideas that influenced much American thought before and into the 20th century was the notion of 'the city on the hill'. When white settlers came to America in the 17th century, they thought of the continent as 'the promised land'. The first Puritans, colloquially called 'the Pilgrims', landed at or near Plymouth Rock in 1620, and thought of themselves as 'God's chosen people' who would found a new city in the 'wilderness' that confronted them. A second, much larger group of Puritans arrived in Massachusetts Bay Colony in the 1630s, and Boston soon became a thriving metropolis. Their mission was to construct a community which would be a 'beacon' to the rest of the world, and which would demonstrate their close relation to God. The result of their special status would be an ideal and inspiring settlement, a model that would show everyone how people ought to live.

▶ Read carefully the passage by Barlowe from 'The First Voyage Made to the Coasts of America' on pages 72–73. What does this description of the New World tell you about the writer's attitudes towards America? Pay particular attention to his treatment of the vegetation, animals and native people. What myths is he encouraging? In what ways do you suppose this ideal will be challenged by the actual experiences of the early settlers in the New World? How would you respond to such contradictions?

Of course from the very start the Puritans had problems and, as Nathaniel Hawthorne later suggested in *The Scarlet Letter* (1850), these first New Englanders soon found that they needed to build prisons as well as churches, law courts as well as merchants' houses. Evidence of sin did not surprise the Puritans, however, for influenced by Calvinist and other Reformation thought, they believed in grace and predestination. That is, they believed that when Adam and Eve ate the apple in the Garden of Eden, all people fell out of favour with God. This 'fall' meant that everyone afterwards was sinful and deserved damnation. Through the agency of Jesus, a few people, God's 'chosen people', would be saved, would go to heaven rather than hell; salvation would occur not because of anything a person had done, but because God had decided to give that person 'grace'. Additionally, the Puritans believed that since God was all-knowing and all-powerful, He certainly knew everything that would happen; there was nothing individual men and women could do to change their destiny.

If grace could not be earned, then, why bother trying to be good, why bother to build a 'city on the hill'? Individual Puritans, hoping that indeed they were among those chosen by God for salvation, looked for signs of His grace. If they could follow His commandments and behave in ways that they learned from the Bible would please Him, then such behaviour was itself a sign of grace, for without God's help, how could they have been other than sinful? What they did – 'works' – could not earn them salvation but were in themselves signs of 'providence', God's favour, as were the positive things that happened to them – for example, happy marriages, healthy children, or success in business.

Such beliefs created tremendous stress in these early Americans. On the one hand, they were hopeful and materialistic, looking for evidence in this world of their status in the next, interpreting wealth and general prosperity as signs that 'God was on their side'. On the other hand, aware of their inherent sinfulness, they felt a deep sense of guilt and responsibility, not only for their own actions but for those of others in their community; they questioned their perceptions and their ability to interpret the world correctly.

While they might not be able to trust their human feelings, they had the Bible to help them to know right from wrong, and all Puritans – women as well as men, servants and slaves as well as merchants and ministers – had an obligation to learn to read the word of God. As a result, these early Americans were highly literate people, keen to understand and to interpret God's messages to them, whether written in the Bible or in 'the book of nature'; that is, in the daily occurrences of life and literally in nature itself, in the seasons and crops and flowers and even in the buzzing of the bees – for all of these were both themselves and signs of something else. Thus these early Americans anxiously interpreted what they read; they were both confident and self-questioning, simultaneously independent and deeply committed to their community.

The American Revolution and American Romanticism

The American Revolution, the War of Independence, has obvious roots in Puritan New England, but also in the Romantic spirit of the 18th century, in the enlightened thinking of such philosophers as Jean Jacques Rousseau and John Locke. The Romantic understanding of human nature was quite different from that of the Puritans. The Romantics felt that the individual was not essentially sinful but basically good or, at least, a 'blank slate' with a great potential for good. Instead of idealising the city as a 'beacon' to others, Romantic thinkers tended to reject urban life for nature, although the rural landscape they had in mind was not the actual 'wilderness' Americans often encountered, the vast stretches of uncultivated forests and prairies whose bears and freezing winters were real threats – as were the Native Americans, driven from their land by the white settlements.

Writers like the 18th century scientist and statesman Benjamin Franklin were much less concerned to see the world symbolically than the Puritans, with their vivid sense of human sinfulness. Franklin could emphasise prosperity for its own sake and stress the obvious material benefits of worldly success. 'Early to Bed and early to rise, makes a Man healthy, wealthy and wise', he wrote, implying that such enterprising and sensible behaviour would result in a 'goodness' that had nothing to do with God's grace, in material achievements that were moral in themselves. Such thinking tended to confuse spiritual and material worth, and later American writers would repeatedly return to this confusion as a fundamental difficulty in American experience. For example, in F. Scott Fitzgerald's (1896–1940) *The Great Gatsby* (1925), the central character, an unscrupulous and pretentious gangster, obviously admires Franklin's work. As a boy, James Gatz makes a schedule for 'self improvement' which includes such resolves as getting up at six in the morning, saving money, practising public speaking, studying electricity and 'needed inventions'. The young Gatsby's reading material – cheap cowboy novels – also suggests 'an extraordinary gift for hope, a romantic readiness' founded on an extremely American self-confidence, a sense that one can achieve anything if one only works hard enough – a conviction Fitzgerald used his novel to question.

Romantic notions of national possibility and individual human potential were at the heart of the American Revolution which, with the Declaration of Independence in 1776, transformed the American Colonies into the United States. But just what was this union of separate states, this new republic? In 1787, the Constitutional Convention defined the nation in political terms with the writing of the U.S. Constitution. Other writers in the first half of the 19th century struggled in different ways to define what it meant to be an American. The Romantic poet and essayist Ralph Waldo Emerson argued that the true American was self-reliant and in tune with nature, that everyone had the power to discover what was true and right.

▶ Robert Frost is often considered a poet whose roots stretch back to early America. Look at 'Fire and Ice' and 'The Secret Sits' on pages 85–86. What Puritan ideas and attitudes can you see reflected in these poems? Do you feel Frost is also responding here to Franklin's emphasis on material prosperity or Emerson's notion of self reliance? Is Frost being serious or ironic in these poems? Do you think he is saying something only about American experience or is he conveying universal truths?

In contrast to Emerson, Nathaniel Hawthorne explored the human capacity for interpretation and questioned the notion of fixed meaning. Melville also revealed an interest in human imperfection and moral confusion in such works as *Moby Dick* and *Billy Budd* (1891). The poet Walt Whitman (1819–1892) in *Leaves of Grass* (1855) offered a vision of humankind and of America which celebrated diversity and resolved apparent contradictions. His particular angle of vision allowed him to write that he was as much the poet of the body as of the soul, that as a poet he contained, gave voice to and celebrated all of America.

▶ What vision of America does Walt Whitman celebrate in sections 16 and 17 of 'Song of Myself' (pages 73–74)? Consider his sentence structure as well as his use of language, detail and point of view. What are the geographic limits of America? What sorts of people are included in Whitman's catalogue of Americans? What do we know about Whitman's speaker? Do you like him? Is he an actual person? What is the speaker's relation to the reader? What is the poet saying about the American experience?

Understandably, for Whitman as for many other American writers, the Civil War (1861–1865) called into question many earlier ideas of nationhood as the North, the Union, struggled with the South, the Confederacy.

The American Civil War

The Civil War was a conflict over power. The North, with its flourishing industrial base and populous cities, had a larger representation in the U.S. Congress, allowing northern states a greater voice in national policy. The issue that divided the nation was state sovereignty, the right of each state to decide internal matters. The problem that brought this issue to the fore was slavery, which seemed necessary to the South, whose farming economy depended on cheap labour. In the face of abolitionist feeling in the North and in an effort to gain greater congressional representation, southern congressmen insisted that new states entering the United States be slave states either on the basis of geography or by a free vote. When the North refused, the South broke away and war followed.

The role of writers in this conflict was important. American authors and lecturers captured public attention by treating the subject of slavery as a moral issue of both race and class, by insisting that black people were human individuals harmed by an oppressive system. When in 1863 President Abraham Lincoln was introduced to Harriet Beecher Stowe, the author of the famous anti-slavery novel *Uncle Tom's Cabin* (1852), he is reported to have said, 'So this is the little lady who made this big war.' (quoted in Forrest Wilson, *Crusader in Crinoline: The Life of Harriet Beecher Stowe*, 1942) Despite his patronising **diction**, Lincoln here calls attention both to the influence of the written word and to Stowe as a female writer. In fact, there were important connections between moral convictions about slavery, American literature and the status of women. Stowe was not only an abolitionist and an established author but a crusader at the forefront of a feminist movement that would eventually result in women's acquisition of the vote in 1920.

When the Civil War ended, the American South was physically and economically ravaged. The legacy of slavery would continue to trouble the nation throughout the 19th and 20th centuries at the same time that the Civil War itself took on particular meaning for the South, symbolising the end of an era. William Faulkner explores these problems throughout his fiction – for example, in *Light in August* (1932) Joe Christmas agonises over the issue of his racial identity, while the Reverend Gail Hightower struggles to understand the significance of the Civil War both for himself and for his community.

The American West

The end of the Civil War also signalled the beginning of a new era, however, as more people moved west and areas which had been territories petitioned for statehood. The newspaper editor Horace Greeley, responding to unemployment in New York City in 1851, urged a geographical solution: 'Go West, young man.' By the time of the publication of *Adventures of Huckleberry Finn* in 1884, however, Mark Twain could only look ironically at the promise of the American West. At the end of this novel, set in the 1840s, Huck says: 'I reckon I got to light out for the Territory ahead of the rest, because Aunt Sally she's going to adopt me and sivilize me and I can't stand it. I been there before.' The possibilities for independent thinking and living that the West offered in the decades before the Civil War were much more limited by the 1880s, and writers at the end of the 19th century had to confront Huck's problem. Familiar with the restrictions and corruption of 'sivilization', symbolised by Mark Twain as the American East (just as Fitzgerald would do later in *The Great Gatsby*), Huck sets out for a place which Mark Twain's readers knew no longer existed, if it ever had, except as a myth. The early Puritans had left Europe for the New World, sailing westward to America, which was for them as much an idea as a physical place. During the nation's formative years, westward exploration and settlement offered new opportunities and represented the chance for individual freedom. The cowboy novels young Gatsby read illustrated these legendary possibilities which persisted in the American imagination. By the 1890s, however, writers recognised that America had 'run out of West', had literally reached the Pacific, and would need to seek meaning not in a geographical fable but in the cities and small towns which lay between the boundaries of its continental shores.

The literary movements of **realism**, **regionalism** and **naturalism** set the scene for American writing in the 20th century.

Setting the scene

- What was the literary atmosphere in 1900?
- What ideas, issues and problems did American writers face at the turn of the century?

Realism and regionalism

By 1900, American writers were engaged in a serious discourse about their responsibilities. The work of Mark Twain and others at the forefront of the literary movement known as realism felt obligated to portray American life as it actually was and not as they might have liked it to be. With such realism came social criticism, and many authors at the turn of the century took this duty as one of their central purposes. For Mark Twain, who developed his art in the context of a tradition of rough American humour, satire was a logical literary tool. One way of reading *Adventures of Huckleberry Finn* is to see it as a social critique which makes fun of those cultural tendencies which Mark Twain disliked and which Huck finally rejects in setting out for the territory. This novel is also a good example of regionalism, a literary movement within realism that encouraged authors to write about material that depended on a particular geographical area, to capture in their work local customs, physical background and speech. Regionalist writing often included vivid depictions of particular experience and explored the meaning of age, race, class and gender as well as region. For instance, Huck tells his story in his own voice. Adopted by the Widow Douglas, the fourteen-year-old finds it difficult to adjust and tells us in his eloquent **vernacular**:

> ... it was rough living in the house all the time, considering how dismal regular and decent the widow was in all her ways ... When you got to the table you couldn't go right to eating, but you had to wait for the widow to tuck down her head and grumble a little over the victuals, though there warn't really anything the matter with them. That is, nothing, only everything was cooked by itself. In a barrel of odds and ends it is different; things get mixed up, and the juice kind of swaps around, and the things go better.

Words like 'victuals' and 'swaps' suggest Huck's lack of education and rural background as does his colloquial 'warn't'; phrases like 'dismal regular' and 'go right to eating' convey Huck's class and character through local American speech. But if his narrator is unsophisticated, Mark Twain certainly isn't, and while Huck's ignorance and honesty may amuse us, the author uses Huck's simple observations to make serious points about society. The widow is a slave owner whose unreflective habit of cooking food separately suggests her support of an oppressive establishment which separates people according to race and class. Mark Twain uses his novel to question conventional ways of thinking and living, suggesting the truth in what Huck knows from experience – that when 'things get mixed up', they 'go better'.

Regionalism, with its emphasis on local colour and ordinary people, encouraged work by male and female writers throughout the country. Focusing on the lives of women, Sarah Orne Jewett (1849–1909) wrote about villagers on the Maine seacoast, while Mary E. Wilkins Freeman (1852–1930) depicted characters from Massachusetts and Vermont, descendants of the colonists in whom 'can still be seen traces of those features of will and conscience ... which characterised their ancestors.' (from the Preface to Mary E. Wilkins Freeman *A Humble Romance and Other Stories*, 1887). Kate Chopin (1850–1904) emphasised the experiences of women who lived in cosmopolitan New Orleans and in the more rural areas of Louisiana, capturing attitudes and speech which reflected the influence of early French settlers in these areas.

▶ Look at Sarah Orne Jewett's description of a New England town in the passage from *The Country of the Pointed Firs* (pages 76–77). What impression do you get of Dunnet Landing? Pay particular attention not only to the details about the village itself but to what Jewett says about Mrs Todd's garden. Consider also her portrait of individual characters. What special 'regional' elements is the author emphasising ?

The best regionalist authors did more than depict local history, values and customs; they used particular experience to examine controversial social and psychological issues. For example, Chopin's important novel, *The Awakening* (1899), explores the frustration of an ordinary woman unable to overcome the limitations her society has placed upon her. Despite her psychic 'awakening', Edna Pontellier cannot escape her given roles, and in the book's final scene, a brilliant psychological study, Edna walks naked into the sea and drowns.

▶ Consider the relationship between the two characters, John and the female speaker, in the passage from Charlotte Perkins Gilman's short story 'The Yellow Wallpaper' (pages 75–76). Why do you suppose the speaker declares that she 'must' write what she thinks and feels? What does writing mean to her? Why would John think her writing 'absurd'? Is this merely an account of a woman going crazy or is Gilman offering us 'social protest' here? What evidence do we have that the speaker is unstable? What aspects of life in late 19th century America might the author be protesting against?

Naturalism

Mark Twain's early work is generally light-hearted and comic; his later writing is often dark, bitter and bleak, for he became angrier about what he saw as America's failures and less confident about humanity's capacity for reform. In rejecting Romanticism and especially sentimentality, literary realists and regionalists laid the foundation for naturalism, a movement whose authors tended to see their characters as victims of social – and even natural and supernatural forces – over which they had little or no control. Frank Norris (1870–1902), Jack London (1876–1916) and Upton Sinclair (1878–1968) wrote about characters who generally struggled in vain against their environment and human limitations. Stephen Crane (1871–1900) succinctly captures the spirit of naturalism in his collection of poetry, *War Is Kind* (1899). Experimenting with **free verse** in poem 96, he writes:

> A man said to the universe:
> 'Sir, I exist!'
> 'However,' replied the universe,
> 'The fact has not created in me
> A sense of obligation.'

▶ There are two speakers in Crane's 'A man said to the universe'. How are they different? What is Crane saying about human beings? Does Crane understand 'the universe' as God or fate? Why do you suppose a poet with Crane's values and attitudes would choose to write in free verse?

Social issues

The literary movements of realism, regionalism and naturalism brought to early 20th century American writing a powerful sense of **irony**, often coupled with a strong commitment to social justice. Garland Hamlin (1860–1940), for instance, was an ardent supporter of feminism, while Theodore Dreiser (1871–1945) in *Sister Carrie* (1900) examined the fate of an unsophisticated farm girl who becomes entangled in the snares of modern urban life. The climate was also right for black writers to argue for racial equality in their own voices. Booker T. Washington (1856–1915) supported practical and gradual advancement for his race in his autobiography *Up From Slavery* (1901), while W.E.B. Du Bois (1868–1963) took a more radical position. Contending in his essay collection *The Souls of Black Folk* (1903) that 'The problem of the 20th century is the problem of the color-line', he demanded the same civil rights for black Americans as those enjoyed by whites.

▶ Compare the passage from Booker T. Washington's autobiography *Up From Slavery* (pages 77–78) with the passage from W.E.B. Du Bois' extended essay *The Souls of Black Folk* (pages 78–79). Can you defend Washington against Du Bois' arguments? What are the main differences between these two men? What sort of future does each imagine for black people in 20th century America?

The 19th century bequeathed to the 20th a rich literary legacy in which **form**, language, content and theme reflected the range and variety of American experience.

American modernism and the 'Roaring Twenties'

- How did American writers respond to the First World War?
- How did they react to the rapid changes during the initial decades of the century?
- How were they shaped by the 'Jazz Age'?
- What were the historical and social conditions of the early modern period?

The First World War

Just as the 20th century needs to be understood as beginning in many ways before 1900, the Roaring Twenties, the Jazz Age with its automobiles, flappers and bootleg liquor, began before 1920. As more than merely a decade, as a way of thinking and a set of experiences, this period starts not with the outbreak of the First World War in 1914, but with America's entry into the conflict in April of 1917.

The United States had mixed feelings about Europe, and President Woodrow Wilson was elected for a second term in 1916 in large measure on the basis of his pledge to keep America out of a war which many saw as having nothing to do with them, as something happening 'over there'. This isolationist attitude was not so much hostile to European and even world problems as it was concerned to define America as a self-reliant nation distinct from the Old World, contained and fulfilled by its own geography and resources, both natural and human.

New technology

With U.S. entry into the conflict, however, Americans embraced the advancements in technology which both threatened individuals and armies and brought people together more rapidly and in new ways. In the 1920s, Calvin Coolidge, who served as President for most of the decade, voiced the spirit of these years by declaring that 'The business of America is business'. The telephone and electricity – which meant not only light bulbs but the radio – entered many American homes, while the cinema with its newsreels became a major form of entertainment throughout the country. The automobile brought about tremendous change by making Americans more mobile than ever before, giving rise to the suburb, and providing or redefining work as well as leisure. As Fitzgerald's treatment of technology in *The Great Gatsby* indicates, automobiles, those speedy green and white and yellow luxuries driven by Gatsby, Jordan and Daisy, could indeed symbolise the pleasure-seeking irresponsibility and self-centredness of a generation and an era. Fitzgerald pointed out in his essay 'Echoes of the Jazz Age'(1931) that in addition to mobility, cars gave young people – especially those of the middle and upper classes and those who lived in cities – a privacy they had never known before, and by 1920, a kiss no longer meant that a proposal of marriage was expected.

Sex and politics

Fitzgerald would go so far as to contend that the Jazz Age in fact 'had no interest in politics at all'. When the war ended in 1918, it was as if America set about concluding its political business and getting on with the pleasures of life. For example, the feminist movement of the preceding century, composed predominantly of radical women and men from the northeastern United States, had had a wide agenda, fighting against abolition and women's disenfranchisement. After the Civil War, the movement had worked for the civil rights of women, children and blacks. Without the support of southern white women, however, it seemed impossible to gather the backing necessary to achieve the vote, a goal that replaced the abolition of slavery, and by the turn of the century the women's movement had made a number of difficult but strategic concessions and alliances. Emphasising the rights of women over those of blacks, they gained the support of many women in the American South. They also broadened their base in the South and Midwest by joining ranks with the conservative Women's Christian Temperance Union. It should not, then, surprise us that two amendments to the U.S. Constitution were passed in 1919 and 1920: one prohibiting the manufacture, transportation and sale of liquor; the other finally granting the vote to women. Ironically, Prohibition, repealed in 1933, probably did little to prevent Americans from drinking and was in part responsible for an enormous rise in organised crime, while the achievement of suffrage deprived feminists of a clear focus. Women would need to wait until the 1960s before they again had a movement to champion their causes.

Yet attitudes towards sexuality, as Fitzgerald noticed, changed significantly in the 1920s. Popular understandings of the theories of Sigmund Freud and Karl Marx caused people to question earlier assumptions about sex and class. Women's fashions of the period illustrate the impact of these new ideas. Before the war, whalebone corsets gave women 'hour glass' figures that emphasised their hips and bosom while making it difficult for them to move easily and even to breathe. At the end of the war, the bandeau replaced the corset, and women's figures altered dramatically: suddenly their chests were flat, their hems went up and their waists came down. Instead of looking like matriarchs, women looked like little boys. They bobbed their hair and the 'flapper' was born.

New forms and new subjects

Such experimentation with new ideas transformed America and influenced its literature in a variety of ways. Edith Wharton (1862–1937), whose novels chronicled the lives of men and women in New York society, was at the height of her career when she published *The Age of Innocence* in 1920. Set in the 1870s, Wharton's book required a great deal of research and explored a world still bound by form and convention. Her vivid and penetrating study of a bygone era was an immediate critical and financial success – serialised chapters received popular acclaim and Hollywood bought the film rights – but Wharton had to struggle against the materialism and superficiality of contemporary readers who trivialised her writing at the same time that they admired it. When her agent urged her to cut the book for serialisation in order to make space for illustrations and detergent advertisements, she refused: 'I cannot consent to have my work treated as prose by the yard.' (quoted in Shari Benstock *No Gifts from Chance: A Biography of Edith Wharton*, 1994). The high praise she received from critics indicates both her achievement and her dislocation. She was favourably compared to Henry James (1843–1916) as well as to the English novelists Joseph Conrad and Jane Austen, and the French short story writer Guy de Maupassant. Of these, only the first two could be claimed as contemporaries, and only James – who settled in England in 1876, having lived most of his life abroad – had been born in America. When Fitzgerald, who much admired Wharton's literary skill as a social chronicler, sent her a copy of *The Great Gatsby* in 1925, the older author was touched, feeling that by the mid-twenties his generation saw her only as 'the literary equivalent of tufted furniture and gas chandeliers'. (quoted in Shari Benstock, above)

▶ Look at Carl Sandburg's 'Salvage' (page 81). What is his attitude towards art and the past? The first and last lines of 'Salvage' are identical; how does the meaning of this sentence change as a result of Sandburg's references to William Morris, the 19th century English artist and designer? What does Sandburg admire about Morris? Why does the poet say that he is glad that Morris is 'a dead man'? On the basis of this poem, what might you conclude about Sandburg's attitude toward the Great War? What do you suppose the poem's title means?

The generation of writers who began their careers in the Jazz Age were social critics of a different kind, eager to experiment with new forms and new subjects. In 1919, Sherwood Anderson (1876–1941) heralded this innovative literature when he published his important novel, *Winesburg, Ohio*, a bold examination of life in a small Midwestern town, unconventionally structured as a series of linked stories. Anderson's men and women struggle to overcome personal and social limitations, trying to realise their individual worth and potential. His explicit treatment of sexuality seemed especially contemporary, even shocking at the time, while his psychological insight seemed very modern: he presents people shaped by unconscious urges and the repression of their desires. Anderson's direct style and unflinching attention to his characters' inner lives give his work a powerful honesty which impressed his contemporaries as both fresh and daring.

Like many authors of this period, Anderson consciously drew on Mark Twain's Huckleberry Finn as a model for his voice and values. Huck's dialect and candour, his lack of sophistication, vital inner life and independent judgement appealed to writers disillusioned with conventional forms and subjects. In 1915, Edgar Lee Masters (1868–1950) had outraged readers with his criticism of small-town America in *Spoon River Anthology*, a work which inspired not only Anderson but Robert Frost (1874–1963) and Sinclair Lewis (1885–1951), whose novels *Main*

Street (1920) and *Babbitt* (1922) satirise the confining patterns and cultural emptiness of provincial American life.

▶ Read the passages from Sinclair Lewis's novel *Babbitt* (pages 83–85). What impression does he convey of the city of Zenith? What are its residents' values? What details, situations, and phrases are especially vivid? Considering the **mood** and **tone** of these passages as well their subjects, do you think Lewis feels essentially positive or negative about American life in the 1920s?

Setting his work in the local cemetery, Masters creates characters who speak about their lives from beyond the grave. His use of specific voices, who address us directly and concisely, indicates another significant element in the literature of the 1920s: a concern with individual speakers who reveal themselves in ways more often associated with stage performances.

Dramatic voices

Until the 20th century, most of the plays produced in America were written by Europeans, and most of these were melodramas, showpieces for touring actors and actresses. Eugene O'Neill (1888–1953) was the first major American dramatist. His early plays were short and realistic, but in the 1920s, he began to experiment with new ways of dramatising his characters' psychology and the complicated dynamics of family life. Influenced by Freud and his European contemporaries as well as by Shakespeare and classical Greek drama, O'Neill brought exciting energy and innovations to the American stage. However, the dramatic voice has a long history in the nation's fiction and poetry, and writers throughout the 1920s continued to use it, exploring its limits and possibilities while building on the rich tradition of first-person literature of the previous century. Huck is not the only figure, after all, to tell his own story: Ishmael tells us *Moby Dick*; Walt Whitman develops a powerful first-person speaker in 'Song of Myself'; Emily Dickinson (1830–1886) experimented with a variety of voices and moods in her verse. 20th century American authors were drawn like their predecessors to the first-person speaker. Nick Caraway tells us Gatsby's story – and thus makes *The Great Gatsby* finally his own story and the story not only of his experiences in the East but of his coming to terms with those experiences through writing about them. T.S. Eliot initially thought of his important poem *The Waste Land* (1922) as an exploration of different voices, and much of his work is dramatic. 'The Love Song of J. Alfred Prufrock' (1915) opens with Prufrock's voice: 'Let us go then, you and I,/ When the evening is spread out against the sky/ Like a patient etherised upon a table'. 'Gerontion' (1920) similarly begins with a character who speaks directly to us: 'Here I am, an old man in a dry month,/Being read to by a boy, waiting for rain.' Eliot's work indeed includes not only essays and poetry but successful plays like

Murder in the Cathedral (1935), his dramatic study of the murder of Thomas à Becket in Canterbury.

Robert Frost (1874–1963) was another modern poet especially interested in dramatic voice. In such poems as 'Mending Wall' (1914) and 'The Death of the Hired Man' (1914) he used dramatic situations in order to examine character, relationships and values at the same time that he depicted, like regionalist writers, a particular place and period, in this case the New England of his own time. Although he had to struggle to establish his career, Frost's work gained an admiring audience in the 1920s; he became so widely regarded that John F. Kennedy asked him to read a poem at his presidential inauguration in 1961. Frost's verse nevertheless offers a stark contrast to Eliot's because of obvious differences in their use of form. To Frost, traditional forms – regular rhyme and **meter** as well as fixed forms such as the sonnet – were essential to poetry. He once said jokingly that writing poetry without such forms was like playing tennis without the net – no fun. More seriously, he argued that modernity was a matter of content rather than formal experiment. His use of American speech patterns, deceptively simple images and natural settings made his work accessible, while his scepticism, occasional bitterness and psychological insight into human character made his work modern. Frost did not seek freedom of form, but in his own words 'the freedom of my material'.

Literary experimentation

Ezra Pound (1885–1972), a dynamic poet who championed the cause of **modernism**, the international movement which advocated innovation in all the arts, found Frost's work 'VURRY Amur'k'n'. Pound was excited early on by Frost's treatment of American subject matter and use of American language, but in his own work Pound moved increasingly towards formal experimentation and obscure, difficult subjects and themes. These were the literary elements he admired in Eliot, who Pound felt had 'trained himself *and* modernised himself *on his own*' (quoted in Humphrey Carpenter *A Serious Character: The Life of Ezra Pound,* 1988).

Modernism encouraged all sorts of innovations in both poetry and prose. Generally rejecting conventional forms, modernist poets often used free verse to express their ideas. Like Pound and Eliot, such writers as Gertrude Stein (1874–1946) and H.D. (Hilda Doolittle, 1886–1961) left America and developed their modernism within an international context. In contrast, Carl Sandburg (1878–1967), Wallace Stevens (1879–1955), William Carlos Williams (1883–1963), Marianne Moore (1887–1972) and E.E. Cummings (1894–1962) were modernist poets who remained in the United States and rooted themselves in American material.

Modernists in both verse and prose explored subjects, such as sexuality and the body, that had previously been 'off limits' or unrecognised, like the unconscious.

▶ Examine Sherwood Anderson's portrait of Alice in the passage from *Winesburg, Ohio* (pages 81–83). In what ways is this passage a psychological study? How does he manage to reveal the tensions within this character? How does he depict the workings of her mind? Can you also read this passage as a piece of social criticism? Why do you think this piece of writing was shocking at the time?

Testing the boundaries of language and trying to reveal the way people really think, Stein reflected on the process of writing and the nature of audience in her long modernist autobiography *The Making of Americans* (1925):

> I am writing for myself and strangers. This is the only way I can do it. Everybody is a real one to me, everybody is like some one else too to me. No one of them that I know can want to know it and so I write for myself and strangers.

Stein's simple language here, most of it monosyllabic, combined with her repetition of sounds and words, forces us to read her prose slowly and carefully to grasp her subtle distinctions and variations of meaning. Reading her work, we need to understand that language is working in a way that may seem difficult to us because it is fresh and original. The satisfaction comes in discovering Stein's peculiar perspective as well as her linguistic cleverness.

The poetry of E. E. Cummings reveals other ways of achieving what Pound advocated when he urged writers to 'make it new'. Playing with capitalisation and word spacing, Cummings wrote poems which in their very appearance on the page strike readers as unusual and modern. In his poem 'in Just–' (1920) he writes:

> ... when the world is mud-
> luscious the little
> lame balloonman
>
> whistles   far   and wee
> and eddieandbill come
> running from marbles ...

Here the poet elides some words ('eddieandbill'), joins others with hyphens, then splits them with a line break; he inserts space in the middle of lines and, by omitting punctuation, refuses the closure we expect at the end of a sentence. Despite these technical surprises, Cummings' subject matter – in this case, children in a city park in springtime – makes his work accessible, while his spirit of playfulness and affirmation are less discomforting than Frost's sharp scepticism.

▶ Look at three short modernist poems: Ezra Pound's 'In a Station of the Metro', H.D.'s 'Oread' and Sandburg's 'Fog' (all on page 80). In what ways are these poems experimental? Consider their subjects and themes as well as their use of language, rhyme, and meter.

Ernest Hemingway

Ernest Hemingway (1899–1961) also developed a modernist voice which depended on both a distinctive style and challenging material. Influenced by his early work as a newspaper reporter, Hemingway's prose is spare and powerful. Rejecting sentimentality and abstractions, he emphasises simple verbs and nouns in sentences with few adjectives or dependent clauses. His subjects and themes are daring, too, as he depicts the lives of men and women threatened by war and violence. He is especially fascinated by the difficulties his characters encounter in trying to define themselves and their relationships when traditional notions of masculinity and femininity no longer apply. Set primarily during and just after the First World War, his first book, *In Our Time* (1925), is made up of a series of stories interspersed with **vignettes**, each related to the other by content, or by theme. The central character, the young Nick Adams, an autobiographical figure who appears in many of the segments, gives this experimental text additional unity. In the following passage, a complete vignette which illustrates Hemingway's style, Nick – or a nameless young man very like him – recalls an experience early in the war:

> We were in a garden at Mons. Young Buckley came in with his patrol from across the river. The first German I saw climbed up over the garden wall. We waited till he got one leg over and then potted him. He had so much equipment on and looked awfully surprised and fell down in the garden. Then three more came over further down the wall. We shot them. They all came just like that.

Hemingway's elementary verbs ('were', 'came', 'saw', 'got', 'had', 'looked', 'fell') are especially forceful as their familiarity contrasts starkly with the horror of this experience. Except for his two uses of 'then', the author avoids transitions, making the brutal events particularly disjointed and disconcerting. The point of view is detached, but the reader suspects that the speaker cannot really be undisturbed by killing Germans. He may initially feel he is 'potting' them as a young boy might hit a target or a bird while out hunting, but Hemingway's simplest sentence here – 'We shot them' – makes clear the narrator's awareness of the awful facts. The vignette's last sentence emphasises, too, that this incident in the garden at Mons, a place we might have expected to be calm and peaceful, involves not only the 'first German' and then 'three more' but 'all' of the others who came over 'just like that'. Through the stripped-down language and the carefully chosen ironic details which convey what happens almost completely from the outside, Hemingway is able to suggest the underlying impact of these events on his young narrator.

Other writers of the period also felt obligated to write honestly about the war as an important event which divided the past from the present, which shaped the values and psychology of their generation. They generally saw the violence of battle and the deaths of millions of men in ironic terms, feeling that young people had sacrificed their lives for the economic and political interests of an older generation. This sense of having been duped and exploited coloured their writing.

▶ Read Ezra Pound's long poem 'Hugh Selwyn Mauberly' (1920). Consider especially sections IV and V. What is the speaker's view of the First World War? What sort of attitudes did the soldiers bring to the battle front, according to Pound? Why do you suppose Pound stresses the idea of lies and lying here? What is the difference in these sections between youth and age? On the basis of Pound's poem, what particular challenges does the First World War present to the young writer in the 1920s?

In both *The Sun Also Rises* (1926) and *A Farewell to Arms* (1929), Hemingway drew on his own experiences as an ambulance driver wounded in Italy to explore the effect of war on young people. All of the characters in *The Sun Also Rises* have been hurt by the war – some of them physically, like the narrator Jake Barnes, and all of them emotionally. Wounded in the groin, Jake is unable to make love to Brett and struggles throughout the novel to define himself as a worthy, creative person. He is haunted by what the war has done to him. Hemingway reveals Jake's thought processes as he tries to settle down for the night:

> Probably I never would have had any trouble if I hadn't run into Brett when they shipped me to England. I suppose she only wanted what she couldn't have. Well, people were that way. To hell with people. ...
> I lay awake thinking and my mind jumping around. Then I couldn't keep away from it, and I started thinking about Brett and all the rest of it went away. I was thinking about Brett and my mind stopped jumping around and started to go in smooth waves. Then all of a sudden I started to cry. Then after a while it was better and I lay in bed and listened to the heavy trams go by and way down the street, and then I went to sleep.

Understandably, the war has made Jake bitter, and here Hemingway gets inside his narrator's head. He shows us how Jake's mind works – thinking and jumping and moving in smooth waves – while conveying the range of Jake's feelings. Later, still thinking about Brett, Jake reflects on his psychological state: 'I thought of her walking up the street and stepping into the car, as I had last seen her, and of course in a little while I felt like hell again. It is awfully easy to be hard-boiled about everything in the daytime, but at night it is another thing.'

Using forbidden language

Hemingway does not hesitate to use the frank and colloquial language natural to his characters, even if it might offend some readers, as indeed it did. In *A Farewell to Arms* one soldier says to another, '"Jesus Christ, ain't this a goddam war?"' but throughout this book Hemingway is forced by his editor to substitute blanks for the vulgar words that his characters really used. For instance, when the narrator, Frederic Henry, an American serving with the Red Cross in the Italian Army, comes upon a wounded soldier, he asks the man, '"What's the matter?"' The soldier responds,'"---- the war."' Occasionally Hemingway resorts to euphemisms to avoid blanks. For example, a disillusioned British major tells Henry that '"If they killed men as they did this fall the Allies would be cooked in another year. He said we were all cooked but we were all right as long as we did not know it. ... The last country to realise they were cooked would win the war."' To placate his editor, Hemingway uses 'cooked' here rather than something stronger, although he insists on having the British major conclude brutally, '"It was all balls."'

Hemingway's omission of certain words and his refusal to substitute more genteel terms can produce an effective modernist staccato. For instance, when later in *A Farewell of Arms* two frightened young women catch a ride with the soldiers, one awkwardly tries to reassure them: '"Don't worry ... No danger of ----. No place for ----."' Here Hemingway's blanks create a kind of horror for both the reader and the young women: the blanks suggest that in war there is no place for love, that love has become something dreadful that soldiers want and that threatens women, something so awful that it cannot even be printed.

Even when forced by propriety to use blanks, Hemingway's prose reveals a frank naturalness and a gritty realism that would have been impossible before the 1920s. We can see a similar sort of breaking of boundaries in E.E. cummings' poem 'i sing of Olaf glad and big' (1931). A conscientious objector compelled to serve in the American armed forces, Olaf, whose Scandinavian name suggests the immigrant farmers of Minnesota, the Dakotas and Nebraska, refuses to join in patriotic affirmation of the war. His colonel and fellow serviceman punish him by thrusting his head in a 'muddy toilet bowl' and beating him with 'blunt instruments'. Olaf sticks to his principles: '"I will not kiss your f.ing flag."' Even when they torture him with 'bayonets roasted hot with heat', Olaf refuses to give in: '"There is some s. I will not eat."' Cummings writes that the American government 'threw the yellowsonofabitch/ into a dungeon, where he died'. The poet is being sardonic when he refers to Olaf as 'the yellowsonofabitch', mocking the cruelty and misperception of those in power, while his use of the word 'dungeon' suggests that imprisoning Olaf is barbaric, an act that the reader might expect in medieval but not in modern times. Cummings' speaker concludes that he hopes to see Christ in heaven 'and Olaf, too' because 'unless statistics lie he was/ more brave than me: more blond than you'. This war protest reverses numerous expectations. For example, it is Olaf who is the hero, not the colonel. Further, at the level of language, we might expect the poem to end with the speaker's saying, to rhyme with 'lie', that Olaf was 'braver than I'; instead, Cummings turns the poem on the reader, making us reflect on our own attitudes towards war, violence and patriotism by pointing out that Olaf was better 'than you'. The fact that the poem was published in 1931 might also surprise us at first, but its date indicates the importance of the issues raised by the war and literature's continuing efforts to come to terms with it.

Stream of consciousness

Authors' use of words previously forbidden in serious writing was only one of many ways of exploring literature's possibilities. Interest in their characters' psychological states led some modernists to begin to experiment with **stream of consciousness**, a form of writing which tried to record the inner processes of thinking and feeling. For example, Hilda Doolittle, who wrote under the pen name H.D., began at this time to write a series of interrelated autobiographical fictions which examined the psychic territory of her characters' thoughts and feelings. In *HERmione*, a novel H.D. wrote between 1926 and 1930, Hermione Gart reflects on her plight as a gifted young woman caught between science and art, between the career her father imagines for her and the art her mother gave up for marriage. Having left university without a degree, she feels confined by conventional life and does not know how to escape:

> Music made conic sections that whirled round in circles but she was no good for music and in Pennsylvania it had never occurred to people to paint green on green, one slice in a corner that made a triangle out of another different dimension. Such painting, it was evident to Her Gart (static, frozen in early summer on a woodpath) must lead to certifiable insanity.
>
> Seeing in a head that had been pushed too far toward a biological-mathematical definition of the universe, a world known to her as Pennsylvania go round and form worlds within worlds (all green) Her Gart said, 'I am certifiable or soon will be.'

Having failed exams in science and mathematics, subjects valued by her astronomer father, Her struggles to imagine an artistic career in America, but feels she is losing her grasp of reality. Through stream of consciousness, H.D. conveys her character's psychological state, showing us what Her is 'seeing in a head that had been pushed too far'.

Gender roles

Like H.D. in this passage, many authors now began to explore gender roles and sexuality both as a way of reflecting the realities of the Jazz Age and as a rebellion against what they saw as old-fashioned attitudes and hypocrisy about the nature of human experience. Dorothy Parker (1893–1967), whose book of verse *Enough Rope* became a bestseller in 1926, captured the spirit of the age in the jazzy rhythms and irreverence of such poems as 'General Review of the Sex Situation':

> Woman wants monogamy;
> Man delights in novelty.
> Love is woman's moon and sun;
> Man has other forms of fun.
> Woman lives but in her lord;
> Count to ten, and man is bored.
> With this the gist and sum of it,
> What earthly good can come of it?

Such jaunty, jazz rhythms, often in combination with the poignant subjects and slower, more serious cadences associated with the blues, reflected the influence of Afro-American culture on American literature during this period.

The Harlem renaissance

Many black writers – as well as black artists, musicians and actors – who began to work at this time associated themselves with the creative movement known as the Harlem Renaissance. Based in a black area of New York City, the movement emphasised Afro-American experience in both the North and the South. It also demonstrated the artistic accomplishments of a variety of voices eager to claim a place for themselves as rightful participants in national culture. For instance, Countee Cullen (1903–1946), in his sonnet 'Yet Do I Marvel' (1925), simultaneously illustrates his concern with the plight of the talented Afro-American in a racist society and, in the poem's form and diction and in its **allusions** to classical mythology, his desire to belong to an international literary tradition:

> I doubt not God is good, well-meaning, kind,
> And did He stoop to quibble could tell why

The little buried mole continues blind,
Why flesh that mirrors him must some day die,
Make plain the reason tortured Tantalus
Is baited by the fickle fruit, declare
If merely brute caprice dooms Sisyphus
To struggle up the never-ending stair ...
Yet do I marvel at this curious thing:
To make a poet black, and bid him sing!

(In Greek mythology Tantalus was offered food which disappeared before he could eat it; Sisyphus was forced to push a boulder to the crest of a hill, but every time he reached the top, the stone rolled to the bottom and he had to push it up again.)

Among other artists of the Harlem Renaissance, Zora Neale Hurston (1891–1960) and Langston Hughes (1902–1967) began their literary careers in the 1920s, but their work, which flourished in the following decade, would be less concerned with a light-hearted treatment of the 'sex situation' than with the more difficult issue of class as well as the problems caused by sexual and especially racial oppression. As Cullen reveals in his sonnet, 'the color line' that concerned W.E.B. Du Bois posed major questions that Americans needed to confront. At least for these black writers, despite what Fitzgerald said, writing was a political act.

The 1930s would make literature more political for nearly everyone. If many American writers in the years after the First World War could avoid politics, the fall of the stock market in 1929 brought about such deep changes in national economics that wine, women and song – bootleg whiskey, flappers and jazz – could no longer mask the more serious issues at the heart of American experience.

The Crash and American disillusionment

- What were the economic and social conditions of the 1930s?
- How did American writers respond to the hardships and challenges of the Great Depression?

The stock market

A careful look at investment practices in the 1920s reveals that the boom years could not last. In retrospect especially, the stock market crash at the end of October 1929 appeared inevitable. Throughout the decade, people bought 'on margin', a system that worked like this: if a share of stock cost $10 on Tuesday, a customer could buy it from a broker for $1, with the understanding that when it went up to $12 on Friday, he would sell it, pay the broker the $9 he owed him, plus a commission of $1, and keep $2 – thereby doubling his investment. But the $9, of course, was a myth, an amount the broker himself vouched for or borrowed from a bank, which was itself engaged in buying 'on margin'. So long as stocks went up, as they did consistently throughout the 1920s, the system worked; when stocks went down as people began to lose faith in such corrupt practices, the market crashed: no one had the $9 to pay the brokers, and the brokers in turn did not have the $9 to pay the banks, and the banks didn't have the $9 to pay their customers, who lined up in droves to withdraw money the banks no longer had. Terrific economic hardship followed, with more than 25 per cent of the labour force out of work at the height of the depression in the early 1930s and no governmental welfare scheme to provide social services or financial benefits.

The New Deal

Franklin Delano Roosevelt ran for President by vowing to offer the people a 'New Deal', and indeed political change occurred as soon as he assumed the office in 1933. Realising his campaign promise, he immediately repealed Prohibition in an effort to curb the illegal liquor trade which had given rise to unprecedented urban crime and local 'gangsters', many of them with Mafia connections, who had infiltrated the political structures in large cities, including New York, Boston and Chicago. Roosevelt also quickly began to set in place government departments and programmes to address the financial problems throughout the country. He closed all banks, calling upon the Treasury department to examine their books and to allow only those in good financial condition to reopen, supplied by Treasury money if necessary. He pushed unemployment legislation through Congress, emphasising relief, training, conservation and construction projects at government expense.

The New Deal's most immediate impact on writers and other artists – painters, musicians and actors – came in 1935 through the new Works Progress Administration (WPA), a government programme which offered employment to an average of two million workers each year until 1941. Many of the evocative photographs of poor people and ravaged communities from Appalachia to California were taken by now famous artists such as Dorothea Lange and Walker Evans, who received their funding from the WPA and its subsidiary, the Federal Writers' Project. Authors such as James Agee (1909–1955), Sterling Brown (1901–1989) and Clifford Odets (1906–1963) were similarly commissioned to document the experience of America during these years, writers who might never otherwise have got started or been able to maintain artistic careers. The WPA encouraged the literature of a period which might have been quite differently represented without this unprecedented funding. Nevertheless, American writers remained aware of the nation's precarious economic condition throughout the decade. All these government projects cost more money than was collected through taxes. The deficit was made up partly by raising taxes and partly by a borrowing scheme based on the selling of government bonds, causing a serious rise in national debt.

Many writers sensed that America had been deluding itself about itself throughout the 1920s. Writing about his own emotional breakdown in the early 1930s, Fitzgerald used financial metaphors to explain a personal depression which simultaneously reflected the country's emotional and moral concerns. In a series of essays published in 1936 under the collective title *The Crack-Up*, Fitzgerald wrote of his own nervous breakdown: 'I began to realise that ... my life had been drawing on resources that I did not possess, that I had been mortgaging myself physically and spiritually up to the hilt ... calling upon physical resources that I did not command, like a man over-drawing at his bank.' He concluded by explicitly linking his personal feelings with the American temper: 'my recent experience parallels the wave of despair that swept the nation when the Boom was over'.

▶ Look at Robert Frost's 'Desert Places' (page 86). What is the nature of the external landscape he describes? What is the nature of the inner loneliness the speaker also talks about? What does the poet mean in the last two lines? This poem is characteristic of Frost in many ways, but its mood may also owe something to the decade in which it was written. In what ways might we consider 'Desert Places' characteristic of the 1930s? In thinking about this question, you may want to compare this work with earlier and later Frost poems, for instance 'Fire and Ice' (page 85) and 'The Gift Outright' (page 86).

Political consciousness

This wave of despair encouraged political consciousness. Interest in the psychoanalytic ideas of Sigmund Freud, first popularised in America in the early 1920s, continued to influence how writers understood themselves and others, but now the socialist ideas of Karl Marx also gained wide public attention. The 1930s, in America as throughout Europe, was a decade of unionisation and political ferment, and many authors felt compelled to take up obviously political subjects and themes, while others commented on the national state primarily through the psychological study of individuals.

In 1929, William Faulkner published his modernist novel *The Sound and the Fury*, a good example of a work whose politics is conveyed through psychological analysis. Told from four different points of view, the narrative recounts the social and psychological dynamics of the Compsons, a Mississippi family defined by loss. This subject pervades much of Faulkner's later fiction and has its source in part in the Civil War, that conflict in which the American South lost not merely politically and economically, but spiritually – it not only lost the war but its idea of itself as a special pastoral world in which women and men, blacks and whites were defined by a stable social order. In his notes to a later edition of the novel, Faulkner made his point explicitly: the various members of the Compson family fail to come to meaningful terms with modern life, while the black community, once the family's slaves, manages to carry on without illusions. Faulkner writes eloquently, 'They endured', a conviction he would hold throughout his life. In *Go Down, Moses* (1941), Faulkner located loss and failure even more deeply in the 'American experience'. Here it is not the Civil War or even slavery which has corrupted the South but the illusion of land ownership. Faulkner reveals, through Isaac McCaslin's struggle to define himself individually and in terms of his family history, that no one can own the land; even the Indians, the Native Americans who were persuaded to sell it for a pittance to the first white people, knew that the land was not theirs to sell. Faulkner thus suggests a complex betrayal, a corruption at the heart of American experience which occurred when European settlers made nature into a commodity. F. Scott Fitzgerald makes the same point towards the end of *The Great Gatsby*; he similarly explores the interrelations between personal loss and national failure in his important novel of this period, *Tender Is the Night* (1933).

Other works in the 1930s were more explicitly political. Clifford Odets' play *Waiting for Lefty* (1935) focuses on a meeting to organise a taxi drivers' strike, while *U.S.A.* (1938), a huge trilogy by John Dos Passos (1896–1970), is, like *The Grapes of Wrath* (1939) by John Steinbeck (1902–1968), a serious leftist fiction which celebrates the working class. As early as *Manhattan Transfer* (1925), Dos Passos had experimented with cinematic techniques to convey the multiplicity and fractured nature of urban life. In the three novels of *U.S.A.* published between 1930 and 1936 (*The 42nd Parallel, 1919* and *The Big Money*), he uses similar modernist language and **syntax** to convey his vision of America. Criticising capitalism and arguing for serious social change, Dos Passos blends fiction and non-fiction, mixing excerpts from newspapers, radio programmes, popular songs and public documents with more conventional depictions of fictional characters. Even the unusual appearance of his work on the page suggests the exciting and radical nature of his political ideas. Here is an example from the end of *The Big Money*:

MARKET SURE TO RECOVER FROM SLUMP

DECLINE IN CONTRACTS

POLICE TURN MACHINE GUNS ON COLORADO
MINE STRIKERS KILL 5 WOUND 40

sympathisers appeared on the scene just as thousands of office
workers were pouring out of the buildings at the lunch hour. As they

raised their placard high and started an indefinite march from one side to the other, they were jeered and hooted not only by the office workers but also by workmen on a building under construction

NEW METHODS OF SELLING SEEN
RESCUE CREWS TRY TO UPEND ILL-FATED CRAFT
WHILE WAITING FOR PONTOONS

He looked 'round an' said to his black greasy fireman
Jus' shovel in a little more coal
And when we cross that White Oak Mountain
You can watch your Ninety-seven roll

I find your column interesting and need advice. I have saved four thousand dollars which I want to invest for a better income. Do you think I might buy stocks?

(The 'Ninety-seven' was a train wrecked on its way from Washington, D.C., to Atlanta, Georgia, in 1903. Several railroad songs chronicled its fate.)

Dos Passos uses **juxtaposition** here to depict and satirise the diverse experience he wants to include in his trilogy. Even in this brief section, he manages to refer to New York (the stock market), Colorado, and White Oak Mountain, located in the Blue Ridge range that stretches through the Carolinas. We can also see here a collage of different, individual voices in the author's use of essentially dramatic material as he attempts, like Walt Whitman before him or like William Carlos Williams in his long poem *Patterson* (1946–1958), to create a national epic which will reflect the variety of American life encompassed by its vast geography.

The influence of the media

The two new rising art forms – radio and 'the movies' – came into their own in the 1930s and had, as *U.S.A.* suggests, a direct impact on literature. Sound came to Hollywood in 1929, expanding the possibilities for sustained and complex narrative feature films, while more homes than ever before, in part through government improvement projects, now had electricity. Roosevelt became the first President to use radio effectively to win popular support, and frequently addressed the nation through informal broadcasts known as 'Fireside Chats', while by the 1930s, nearly every American town had its own movie theatre, whose offerings regularly changed twice a week. This was the era of child stars, like Judy Garland and Shirley Temple, and of musical extravaganzas like Busby Berkeley's film *Gold Diggers of 1933*. The Depression encouraged the nation to escape its troubles through such distractions and fantasies as well as through the more serious 'entertainment' offered by radio and cinema. The government subsidised radio plays and movies as well as literature, and during this period many established writers spent at least part of their careers in Hollywood. Fitzgerald worked on numerous film scripts, as did Faulkner (with greater success) on such movies as *The Big Sleep*, an adaptation of Raymond Chandler's novel, and *To Have and Have Not*, based on the novel by Hemingway.

Thus, directly and indirectly, movies influenced literature throughout the decade at the same time that literature influenced the movies. *Tender Is the Night* illustrates this rich cross-fertilisation: one of the central characters, Rosemary Hoyt, is a movie star, who in the course of the novel encourages the male **protagonist**, Dick Diver, to take a screen test. Beyond the level of character and incident, film informs the language of the novel, many of whose metaphors derive from cinema: the book's first section is entitled 'Rosemary's Angle', while at a crucial point in the narrative, Rosemary turns to Dick and says, '"Oh, we're such *actors* – you and I."'

The struggle to earn a living

Some writers were lucky enough to have established their careers before the Crash, although even such a popular writer as Fitzgerald was not able to hold his audience. While Hollywood provided an additional source of income for some authors, others, such as Eliot, Pound and H.D., continued with lives established abroad where, although they could not escape the atmosphere of the Depression, they could at least live more cheaply. Still other writers divided their careers between literature and more mundane jobs, although journalism, an alternative source of income for many authors, was also more difficult during the Depression. Marianne Moore, who worked in the 1920s as an editor at the important *avant garde* magazine *The Dial*, lost her position when the journal stopped publication in 1929. William Carlos Williams was luckier: he worked as a doctor throughout his life. However, while his poetry was enriched by the individual lives that this profession revealed to him, his work as a physician demanded a great deal of time and energy, making writing sometimes very difficult. Wallace Stevens had a career in an insurance company and, like Williams, divided his life between literature and more prosaic work, writing poetry only at night and during his summer holidays. Stevens, however, had little interest in artistic causes or in literary circles or even in politics, and seems not to have been frustrated by a quiet and conventional life in Hartford, Connecticut. His poetry during the 1930s as throughout his literary career reflects his commitment to technique, as well as his view of meaning as a highly individual matter, as in his 'Thirteen Ways of Looking at a Blackbird' (1931). In this poem Stevens offers, without judgement, thirteen different instances of or references to blackbirds in as many stanzas, but he never defines exactly what blackbirds signify – which is perhaps his point. In stanza IV, for instance, he writes:

A man and a woman
Are one.
A man and a woman and a blackbird
Are one.

In stanza IX, he adds the following to our sense of the variety of meanings suggested by the perception of a blackbird:

When the blackbird flew out of sight,
It marked the edge
Of one of many circles.

In stanza XIII, he ends his poem:

It was evening all afternoon.
It was snowing
And it was going to snow.
The blackbird sat
In the cedar-limbs.

▶ Compare Wallace Stevens' 'The Death of a Soldier' (page 87) with Ezra's Pound's depiction of soldiers in 'Hugh Selwyn Mauberley'. What differences in mood and tone do you notice? What might account for these differences?

Black writers

Other writers, notably black men and women, felt increasingly isolated and disenfranchised in the 1930s. The sense of community and optimism that had characterised the Harlem Renaissance in the 1920s gave way in the following decade to a more political and agitated mood, which nevertheless encouraged Zora Neale Hurston's best work, *Their Eyes Were Watching God* (1937), a compelling novel about an African-American woman's search for identity and independence. Trained as an anthropologist, Hurston could find no support for her research during the Depression and devoted her energies to her writing. Her compelling novel is both a woman's narrative (her protagonist Janie Crawford tells her own dramatic story to her best friend Pheoby Watson) and a vivid, often critical depiction of class and gender relations in a southern black community. Janie begins by telling Pheoby about her early childhood: '"Ah ain't never seen mah papa. And Ah didn't know 'im if Ah did. Mah mama neither. She was gone from round dere long before Ah wuz big enough tuh know. Mah grandma raised me. Mah grandma and the white folks she worked wid."' Janie tells how '"Ah was wid dem white chillun so much till Ah didn't know Ah wuzn't white till Ah wuz round six years old."' When a photographer takes their picture, the children look at it carefully, but after 'everybody got pointed out there wasn't nobody left except a real dark little girl with long hair standing by Eleanor. Dat's where Ah wuz s'posed to be, but Ah couldn't recognise that chile as me. So Ah ast, "where is me? Ah don't see me."' Everyone laughs; then the white children's mother points out, '"Dat's you, Alphabet, don't you know yo' own self?"' Janie explains:

> Dey all useter call me Alphabet 'cause so many people had done named me different names. Ah looked at de picture a long time and seen it was mah dress and mah hair so Ah said:
> 'Aw, aw! Ah'm colored!'
> Den dey all laughed real hard. But before Ah seen de picture Ah thought I wuz just like the rest.

Hurston's use of authentic dialect and humour here made some of her contemporaries feel that she was not championing her race, not producing the sort of 'universal' literature that Du Bois called for, but *Their Eyes Were Watching God* is a masterpiece which draws on the American **traditions** of regionalism and local colour in celebrating an individual's struggle for selfhood within a particular American time and place. Ironically, Hurston's work was entirely out of print by the time of her death in 1960; the 1930s and early 1940s were not a good time for a black female writer to find or sustain an audience. Unable to establish herself as either an anthropologist or a writer, she spent the last decade of her life working as a domestic servant in Florida.

Other black writers did manage to survive the Depression. Langston Hughes, drawing like Hurston on the oral traditions and distinctive experiences of Afro-American culture, became known in the 1930s as 'the bard of Harlem', involving himself in radical politics as well as in literature, writing plays and poetry throughout the period. Consciously recalling Walt Whitman – and specifically his famous poem 'I hear America Singing' (1860) – Hughes wrote 'I, Too' in 1932:

> I, too, sing America.
>
> I am the darker brother.
> They send me to eat in the kitchen
> When company comes,
> But I laugh,
> And eat well, and grow strong.

Tomorrow,
I'll sit at the table
When company comes.
Nobody'll dare
Say to me,
'Eat in the kitchen,'
Then.

Besides,
They'll see how beautiful I am
And be ashamed –

I, too, am America.

The implied threats in this poem ('I ... grow strong', 'Nobody'll dare ...') are less an expression of anger than of confidence in what Hughes insists will surely happen in time, 'Tomorrow'. Hughes appears certain that in due course white America will recognise black worth ('They'll see how beautiful I am') and realise the wrong in racial oppression, in fact 'be ashamed'.

Class and economic oppression

Hughes' commitment to racial issues also involved him in the problem of oppression more generally, and like many writers and intellectuals during the 1930s, he was interested in the socialist experiment in Russia. The American Communist Party made racial justice an important part of its programme, championing an ideal of working-class solidarity that crossed 'the color line' and attracted many literary figures who, if they did not actually join the party, attended meetings and subscribed to many of its principles. Like the renowned black singer Paul Robeson, Hughes visited the Soviet Union in the 1930s. Similarly, Dorothy Parker declared herself a communist, taking an early stand on that basis against fascism and Nazi Germany, while Dos Passos and Genevieve Taggard (1894–1948) wrote for the American Communist journal *The New Masses*. Taggard in fact saw poetry as a means for political change, as the following excerpt from her 'Definition of Song' (1935) makes clear:

Singing is best, it gives right joy to speech.
Six years I squandered, studying to teach,
Expounding language. Singing is better,
Teaching the joy of song, not teaching the letter ...

Although she earned her living as a university lecturer, Taggard saw poetry ('singing') as a more powerful medium than teaching for bringing people together. An educated woman married to a reporter for Tass, the Soviet News Agency, Taggard was able to express her radical ideas from a position of social and economic security. Most writers, black and white, male and female, were not so lucky.

It is hard to make a living from literature even in the best of times; the conditions in America in the 1930s made it impossible for many writers. Sterling Brown, a teacher and scholar deeply committed to Afro-American culture, stopped writing poetry in the middle of the decade when his publishers found they could not afford to print his second book *No Hiding Place*. Other aspiring authors – some of whom we know about and many more who, because of lack of opportunity, have disappeared from history – found the Depression an insurmountable barrier to their literary work. Tillie Olsen (b. 1913) writes poignantly about her own difficulties. Born into poverty in the rural Midwest, Olsen struggled to write as a young woman throughout the 1930s, finally giving up both her writing and her desire for an education to marry and raise a large family. The feminist movement in the 1960s reactivated her literary ambitions. She went on to write, in essays and short stories, about what happens when artistic aspirations, particularly for women, are 'silenced'. Coming upon pages and notes which she had nearly forgotten and thought were destroyed, Olsen published in 1974 a fragmentary novel, a short segment of which had been published in a magazine forty years earlier. Taking her title from Whitman's poem of the same name, a Native American word meaning 'lament' for what is lost, she called her book *Yonnondio* and subtitled it *From the Thirties*. The narrative tells the story of the Holbrooks, a family struggling against dire poverty, who migrate from a coal mining town to a farm, then to an industrial city in search of a better life. Using the point of view of Mazie, a girl of seven, Olsen writes towards the end of the novel about the difficulties that occur after Anna, the mother, while still nursing her fourth child, has a miscarriage. Seriously ill, Anna refuses to rest. When her husband Jim comes home from his work in the sewers, he says, '"Don't get me mad now ... You know you shouldn't be up."' Anna responds:

> 'And shouldn't I?' pulling herself erect, 'and shouldn't I? Let the dirt stay, let the kids run wild and not a decent stitch on 'em, let there be no making do on the money, I shouldn't be up. *Don't touch me!* ... Don't sweet Anna me. Who's to do it if I'm not up? Answer. *Who?* Who's to ... look out for ...' Gasping hoarsely. 'Who's to care about 'em if we don't? Who?'

An argument follows, and Anna collapses on her bed, repeating, 'the children':

Over and over, broken: 'the children. What's going to happen with them? How are we going to look out for them? O Jim, the children. Seems like we can't do nothing for them in this damn world.'

The incident concludes with Mazie's perspective:

It is over. There is reconciliation in the house where your mother lies weeping; not hearing the *I'll spade up the garden and tomorrow, payday, we'll get seeds. We'll work things out, you'll see, don't take on so*; hearing only the attempt at comfort. And now your father lies beside her, stroking and kissing her hair, silently making old vows again, vows that life will never let him keep.

In her subject, language and characterisation here, Olsen vividly chronicles the disillusioning period which lasted more than a decade, which in fact stretched from 1929 when the stock market crashed until America entered the Second World War at the very end of 1941.

► Look at the passages from Dos Passos' *The Big Money* (pages 33–34), Olsen's *Yonnondio* (pages 39–40) and the poems by Hughes (pages 37–38) and Taggard (page 38). Now look at the passage from E.L. Doctorow's *World's Fair*, a novel written in the 1980s but set at the end of the 1930s (pages 96–97). What elements in this material from the 1930s does Doctorow's protagonist capture in his essay 'The Typical American Boy'? What elements important to those authors writing in the 1930s does Doctorow's speaker omit? What role does irony play in these poems and passages? Consider not only the speakers' and the authors' irony, but the irony we bring to these works as readers with a sense of later events, with an awareness of history which writers in the 1930s could not have known about.

The post-war world

- How did American writers respond to the Second World War?
- In what ways does the literature of the post-war period confront and record the issues of the 1950s and 1960s?

The Second World War

The United States approached the Second World War with many of the same attitudes that it had brought to the First. While Roosevelt developed and consolidated ties with Latin America and Canada, his 'Good Neighbor Policy' was confined to countries on America's side of the Atlantic. Most Americans favoured 'Isolationism', a policy which reflected the nation's desire to focus on domestic issues and to keep out of what it saw as 'foreign entanglements'. Even when Germany invaded Poland in September 1939, most Americans did not feel the situation was so serious as Roosevelt and many intellectuals, among them many American Jews, believed. The fall of France in June of 1940 seriously challenged the country's isolationist mood, and Roosevelt began actively to support the Allies by supplying Britain with ships and other war supplies. In September of 1940, the United States adopted its first peacetime 'draft', but it was not until 7 December 1941, when the Japanese bombed the U.S. Pacific Fleet in Pearl Harbor, Hawaii, that America entered the war. Roosevelt addressed Congress in a speech simultaneously broadcast on the radio. In memorable rhetoric, he declared 7 December 'a date that will live in infamy'.

With the shift to a war economy, America finally emerged from the Depression and turned its emotional energies towards the conflicts in Europe and the Far East. Most serious literature about the war, however, was not written during the turmoil but afterwards. Norman Mailer (b. 1923), who served in the Pacific, wrote his first book, *The Naked and the Dead*, in 1948. Like Herman Melville in *Moby Dick*, Mailer used his war novel to create a microcosm of society, but unlike Melville, whose crew on the *Pequod* represented the world, Mailer's platoon represented America, containing a New York Jew, an Italian-American, a black southerner, a country boy from Texas. The author captured battle scenes in vivid detail and language, while the work as a whole allowed characters to debate ideas especially important at the time, questioning the value of violence, the purposes of war, the nature of manhood, and the identity of America and Americans in world turmoil.

A crisis in confidence

A very different sort of writing emerged in the immediate post-war years. Despite the disillusion that characterised the inter-war period, writers in the 1930s, even as they chronicled a down-and-out America, still seemed to feel a confidence in the power of literature to bring about social change, if only by recording realities as they saw them. Post-war literature contained an angrier, more critical and even bitter analysis of American society. Tennessee Williams' (1911–1983) play, *The Glass Menagerie* (1945), clearly reveals these attitudes at the same time that it eloquently evokes the pre-war period in which it is set. The play takes place in Saint Louis, Missouri, in the late 1930s, and tells the story of Tom Wingfield, the work's autobiographical narrator, who wants to be a writer but is bound emotionally to his mother Amanda and sister Laura. Desperate to leave home but aware that the women depend on his income from menial labour in a shoe factory, he stays as long as he can, reluctant to follow the model of his father, a worker for the telephone company who, long before the play opens, has deserted the family by falling 'in love with long distances' and tripping 'the light fantastic out of town'.

All three of the drama's central characters escape reality through fantasy. Amanda deludes herself about her status as a lady of the old South, repeating to her children the irritating story of the many 'gentlemen callers' who once sought her hand. Crippled by polio, Laura has little confidence and retreats to the fragile world of the play's title, represented by her menagerie of tiny glass animals. Tom escapes through reading and writing poetry (his fellow workers call him 'Shakespeare'), by going to the movies, and finally literally by joining the Merchant Marines at the drama's end. But there is poignant irony in Tom's 'escapes'. He may see fantasies on the cinema screen, but he also sees newsreels which document the rise of fascism in Italy and Germany as well as the civil war in Spain. Joining the Merchant Marines allows him to escape his family physically, but he remains psychologically tied to them. Additionally, the recruitment posters' promises – that he would 'see the world' – must be understood, from the perspective of 1945 when audiences first saw the play, as ironic indeed, for the 'adventure' he sought in joining the military becomes his direct participation in the brutal war the newsreels foreshadowed. Even writing is no escape: Tom tells us from the start that the play is 'memory', and as he 'writes' the play which he narrates, we are reminded of the seriousness of literature, its capacity to convey realities and to bring both writer and reader unavoidably face-to-face with difficult facts and feelings and themes.

Arthur Miller

Arthur Miller (b. 1915) was another playwright who began his career just after the war. His first play, *All My Sons* (1947), recounts the story of Joe Keller, who during the war knowingly shipped damaged aeroplane parts for financial gain. In a misguided effort to secure material success for himself and his family, Keller risks the lives of others and even endangers the American war effort.

Selfishness and materialism in an increasingly urban and technological world become important subjects in American literature after the war, as the country prospers and the market is flooded with goods. Individuals, in turn, are often presented as alienated and adrift as traditional values and earlier ways of relating to others seem no longer to apply. This was the era of 'the baby boom', as families were encouraged, after the deprivations not only of the war but of the Depression which preceded it, to have children and to acquire possessions now produced in abundance by factories no longer making guns and bullets and warships. The technological advances achieved at a great rate during the war were now turned to peacetime purposes: television, for example, came on the market during the early 1950s; this was the era of the dishwasher, the second car, the suburbs. With the advent of the atom bomb, the post-war period also became the Cold War era. Russia, which had seemed to offer such a promising socialist alternative before the war, was now 'the Red Menace' with a bomb of its own. Children in schools throughout the nation routinely participated not only in fire drills but in air raid drills, as if putting their heads under their desks could protect them from a nuclear attack or the poisonous fallout that would inevitably follow.

A new academic discipline, sociology, the study of the psychology of groups, came into being, and David Riesman's important study, *The Lonely Crowd* (1951), discussed the problems facing post-war America in terms of 'inner directedness' and 'other directedness', in terms of whether one was more or less motivated to think and feel and act independently of others or on the basis of what other people thought and felt and did. While Riesman did not argue than anyone was totally inner- or totally other-directed, clearly inner direction was old-fashioned and more typical of an earlier era, while other direction, as people responded to mass advertising and 'peer pressure', was more typical of the age.

Miller's masterpiece, *Death of a Salesman* (1949), reveals just these conflicts in the character of Willy Loman, whose desire to be not merely liked but 'well liked' leads to his breakdown. Committed to a life of commerce, Willy cannot understand the failure of his ideals, which are the ideals of a nation, in fact the 'American Dream', the delusion that the achievement of material prosperity will bring happiness at the same time that it is evidence of moral superiority. Just when his refrigerator, bought on the instalment plan, is nearly paid for, it is simultaneously falling apart. With the mortgage almost paid off, the Lomans' house needs repair. The garden has been overshadowed by the city built up around it: the tree in the garden where his boys once played has withered and died, while the seeds Willy pathetically plants cannot grow in the shadow of the surrounding apartment buildings. His sons, who initially took on their father's values with enthusiasm, now lead empty and corrupt lives: Biff cannot make it even when, following Horace Greeley's famous advice, he tries to work as a ranch hand out West, while Happy repeatedly fails to move up in the corporate world or to form meaningful personal relationships. We never learn what Willy sells; in fact, he sells himself, making a living on 'a smile and a shoe shine', and is never a very good salesman. Biff says poignantly, at the drama's end, his father 'had the wrong dreams'. Thus Miller makes clear that Willy's failure is not an individual matter but a larger problem of the failure of the American Dream.

This sort of criticism of American life and values gave the literature of the 1950s and 1960s a sharper edge than earlier writing. In his speech accepting the Nobel Prize for Literature in 1950 for his anti-racist novel *Intruder in the Dust* (1948), Faulkner could choose the same word he had used earlier, insisting optimistically that even in the post-war world of the atom bomb, humankind would not only 'endure but prevail', yet his confidence belonged to an earlier era. Mailer's vision of wartime America – in which East and West, North and South, urban and rural, black and white, eventually worked together with singleness of purpose in one unit fighting against a defined external enemy – could not last in a period characterised by race, class and gender division and diversity of experience. Miller, as a New York Jew, came to write increasingly out of his own experience, no matter how universal his themes. Williams, too, as a homosexual from the South, anchored his work in southern experience and the problem of the individual who could not fit in.

Fear of communism

Socialism, and specifically communism as represented by the Soviet Union or the American Communist Party, seemed a real threat to the ideas many Americans held about their country. Most writers and other intellectuals, with their scepticism about the American Dream and materialism more generally, came to be seen as subversive in their minority viewpoints. In the early 1950s, Senator Joseph McCarthy claimed to have a list of 'card-carrying Communists' whose 'Red' sympathies threatened national security and the American way of life. In his role as head of the House Un-American Activities Committee (HUAC), he began a 'witch hunt' that targeted writers and artists, especially those connected with the theatre or Hollywood, who he felt had the most public influence. Intellectuals were called upon to 'confess' their own participation in the Communist Party and were encouraged to bargain for immunity from prosecution by 'naming names' of others they knew to be involved or implicated. Most people called before the committee took what they felt was the only honourable position and, despite serious risks, refused to testify. This atmosphere of paranoia reflected the fears of the nation as the McCarthy 'trials' were broadcast on television. Miller, himself convicted of contempt of Congress when called before HUAC in 1957, wrote a play about the witch trials in 17th-century Massachusetts, *The Crucible* (1953), which can be read as a response to the moral corruption and hysteria he saw in America during this post-war period. Despite repeated appeals, Julius and Ethel Rosenberg, New York Jews convicted of passing secrets to the Soviet Union, became in 1953 the first U.S. citizens ever put to death for wartime spying. Referring to this incident of alleged treason, Sylvia Plath (1932–1963) evoked the decade's claustrophobia in her autobiographical novel, *The Bell Jar* (1963). Her account of her own descent into madness begins: 'It was a queer, sultry summer, the summer they electrocuted the Rosenbergs, and I didn't know what I was doing in New York.'

▶ Read Adrienne Rich's poem 'For Ethel Rosenberg' (pages 92–95). Rich focuses here, in a poem written twenty seven years after the event, on Ethel Rosenberg's experiences. In her poem Rich italicises phrases and statements reported at the time in newspapers. How else does she explicitly set this poem in the context of the public events and personal experiences of that summer? What does this poem tell us about life in 1950s America? Why do you suppose the poet says that she has 'held her at arm's length till now'? How are Rich and Ethel Rosenberg different? How are they similar? Why is Rosenberg so important to Rich?

The civil rights movement

Black people, who throughout the war had been drafted to fight and die for their country just as white people had, were less willing now to accept a segregated America and, like their white brothers and sisters, felt they had a right to their share of post-war prosperity. In 1954, the Supreme Court made a decision which compelled integration throughout the United States, a law whose immediate impact was felt in American schools. The 1950s was the beginning of the race and class conflict that would become known as the civil rights movement, and writing by black authors reflected these social tensions with more anger and bitterness than their predecessors. Richard Wright (1908–1960) heralded this more forceful stance with the publication of *Native Son* in 1940. This novel tells the story of Bigger Thomas, a black boy who turns to shocking violence as a result of poverty and racial prejudice. Prompted by his frustration with oppression and exploitation to follow a tradition of American expatriates, Wright left America to live in France in 1947. His work influenced later black writers such as Ralph Ellison (1914–1994) and James Baldwin (1924–1987). Ellison's most important novel, *Invisible Man* (1952), is a complex work in which his black, first-person speaker recounts his life from a position of threatening retreat and social invisibility. Baldwin, who also left America to live in France in 1948, explores in his fiction, such as *Giovanni's Room* (1955) and *Another Country* (1962), the disenfranchisement of characters who suffer oppression both because of their colour and their homosexuality. Baldwin is perhaps most admired, however, for his protest essays in such collections as *Notes of a Native Son* (1955) and *The Fire Next Time* (1963).

Gwendolyn Brooks (b. 1917) began her literary career with novels and poetry which harkened back to an earlier ideal of a peaceful, integrated society, but in the 1960s, a decade whose activist politics made many intellectuals more militant, she began to see herself as a black feminist leader and to write directly for a black audience and to publish her work only with black presses. Her poem 'Paul Robeson' (1970) recalls the career of the singer and political activist who began in the 1930s by performing songs that white people were comfortable hearing from a black man, such as 'Old Man River' from Jerome Kern's 1927 musical *Show Boat* or 'nigger ditties' with titles like 'The Little Piccaninny's Gone to Sleep' or 'You Didn't Oughta Do Such Things'. By the late 1940s, however, Robeson, devoting his energies to political causes, was recording less and choosing a different repertoire, having resolved not to offer his audiences any more 'pretty lullabies'. Brooks reveals her admiration for Robeson's courage and purpose in her poem:

That time
we all heard it,
cool and clear,
cutting across the hot grit of the day.
The major voice.
The adult voice
forgoing Rolling River,
forgoing tearful tale of bale and barge
and other symptoms of an old despond.
Warning, in music-words
devout and large,
that we are each other's harvest:
we are each other's
business:
we are each other's
magnitude and bond.

The Beats

Another sort of protest occurred in the work of writers known as the Beats. Disassociating themselves from mainstream America and conventional middle class values, such authors as Jack Kerouac (1922–1969), Lawrence Ferlinghetti (b. 1919) and Allen Ginsberg (1926–1998) advocated spontaneity while objecting to convention in both life and literature. Located in San Francisco and in New York City's Greenwich Village, this bohemian group began to experiment with language and form and, foreshadowing the 1960s, with drugs. 'Dropping out' was a phrase which came to describe this sort of protest. A popular novel, *The Catcher in the Rye* (1951) by J.D. Salinger (b. 1919), explored this process through the story of Holden Caufield, a young man who, rejecting conventions which he finds 'phony', leaves school and travels to New York City in an effort to understand himself and to find meaning in his life. In the end, Holden comes to accept both his own weaknesses and life's pain and ugliness. The Beats were more brutal in their criticism and more experimental in their use of language. In 'Howl' (1956), Ginsberg reflected on America's failure to fulfil its promise:

I saw the best minds of my generation destroyed by madness,
starving hysterical naked,
dragging themselves through the negro streets at dawn looking for
an angry fix ...
who were expelled from the academies for crazy & publishing
obscene odes ...

who lounged hungry and lonesome through Houston seeking jazz or
sex or soup, and followed the brilliant Spaniard to
converse about America and Eternity, a hopeless task ...
who burned cigarette holes in their arms protesting the
narcotic tobacco haze of Capitalism ...
who bit detectives in the neck and shrieked with delight in policecars
for committing no crime but their own wild cooking
pederasty and intoxication ...
who balled in the morning in the evenings in rosegardens and the
grass of public parks and cemeteries scattering their
semen freely to whomever come who may ...
who scribbled all night rocking and rolling over lofty
incantations which in the yellow morning were stanzas of gibberish ...
who sang out of their windows in despair, ... cried all over the street,
danced on broken wineglasses barefoot smashed
phonograph records of nostalgic European 1930s
German jazz finished the whisky and threw up groaning
into the bloody toilet, moans in the ears and the blast
of colossal steamwhistles ...
and rose reincarnate in the ghostly clothes of jazz in the goldhorn
shadow of the band and blew the suffering of America's
naked mind for love into an eli eli lamma lamma
sabacthani saxophone cry that shivered the cities down
to the last radio
with the absolute heart of the poem of life butchered out of their
bodies good to eat a thousand years.

('eli eli lamma lamma sabacthani' is Ginsberg's transliteration of the Hebrew of Christ's words on the cross: 'My God, my God, why hast thou forsaken me?')

In one long free-verse sentence reminiscent of Walt Whitman in form and scope, Ginsberg here 'howls' his lament for those promising young creative writers of his generation who found no place for themselves in America. Ginsberg's images are intended to shock, as he struggles to express in fresh, new terms the brutal realities as well as the literary potential of his time. Alienated, the autobiographical characters in his poem traverse the country from 'Harlem' to the 'West Coast', from Canada to Mexico looking for community, love, health and peace. Taking drugs and drinking too much, wildly seeking sexual partners and protesting against violence, racism, technology and commercialism, the poets in 'Howl' are driven mad, 'butchered', by a nation that does not value them, yet they are not destroyed. Instead, inspired by the spirit if not by the reality of America, they rise again, like Christ, to write poems for 'love' of the very America that rejects them.

The search for identity

Other writers tried to make sense of the post-war world by looking for an American identity in terms of history. John Berryman (1914–1972) wrote a long dramatic poem, 'Homage to Mistress Bradstreet' (1953), in which the autobiographical speaker engages in a dialogue with the 17th-century American poet Anne Bradstreet. The speaker identifies with Bradstreet as a fellow rebel alienated from her community, writing 'We are on each other's hands/ who care. Both of our worlds unhanded us.' Robert Lowell (1917–1977) wrote about his own New England past in such poems as 'The Quaker Graveyard in Nantucket' (1946) and 'For the Union Dead' (1964), in which he reflected on the American Civil War as memorialised in a modern Boston characterised by carparks and an abandoned aquarium. Lowell focuses on a regiment of black soldiers whose 'monument sticks like a fishbone/ in the city's throat': ironically, most of them died 'Two months after marching through Boston', while in the present the speaker sees on television 'the drained faces of Negro school-children' caught in the civil rights conflict.

▶ Read Allen Ginsberg's 'A Supermarket in California' (pages 87–88). Why do you suppose he writes that he has been thinking about Walt Whitman? Why does he call Whitman in the last line 'dear father'? Look carefully at the passages from Walt Whitman's 'Song of Myself' as well as at his poem 'Native Moments' (pages 74–75). In what ways is Ginsberg's poem a response to Whitman's work? Consider form as well as content. What does Ginsberg mean by his final question? Look back at the extract from Ginsberg's 'Howl'. How has America changed in the century between 1855, when Whitman wrote 'Song of Myself', and 1955? What specific evidence of these changes do we have in these poems? Is America in Berkeley, California, in any way still Whitman's America? Is Ginsberg's poem angry or sad? Is it nostalgic? hopeful? What problems is Ginsberg facing here as a writer in America?

The main regional responses in post-war literature, however, came not from New England but from two other parts of the country: the South and New York City. Such writers as Truman Capote (1924–1984) and Carson McCullers (1917–1967) wrote, like Tennessee Williams, about their experiences in the American South, defining their often grotesque characters within a particular time and place. Another southern writer, Harper Lee (b. 1926), in her autobiographical novel *To Kill a Mockingbird* (1960) wrote explicitly about racial tensions from the point of view of a young white girl, Scout, who must come to terms not only with the prejudices of her town in Alabama but with what it means to be a female child in a world dominated by adult men. McCullers explores similar themes in *The Member of the Wedding* (1946), an autobiographical narrative she wrote first as a novel and then as a play. In this work, set during the summer of 1944, the protagonist, thirteen-year-old Frankie, longs to find 'the we of me', a community to which she belongs. Initially, she wants to be a 'member of the wedding', to join her brother and his new bride on their honeymoon. She vacillates throughout the narrative between wanting to be a child and a woman. At one point, eating in the kitchen with her black housekeeper Bernice and her seven-year-old cousin John Henry, she crawls into Bernice's lap; later, she dresses up and goes out at night, casually and dangerously picking up a soldier. At the conclusion of the narrative, she is accepted by a group of popular girls whose femininity and superficiality she had earlier scorned, but this ending is no simple resolution of an adolescent crisis. McCullers makes clear that Frankie's dream of someday travelling abroad with her newly found best friend is naive in the context of a Europe ravaged by war and a world which must face the threat of annihilation posed by the devastation of Hiroshima and Nagasaki.

New York writers, like Arthur Miller and Norman Mailer, tended to be Jews who wrote out of their urban experience. Such writers as Bernard Malamud (1914–1986), Saul Bellow (b. 1915), and Philip Roth (b. 1933) explored the lives of characters who were often marginalised by their Jewishness in cities which enclosed them, shutting them into narrow worlds and preventing alternative ways of thinking or being. Malamud's novel *The Assistant* (1957) tells the depressing story of the conflict between two grocery workers, a Jewish shop owner and his Gentile assistant, who fail to relate to one another. In *The Fixer* (1966), Malamud continued to explore the tensions between Jew and Gentile, focusing on a 'fixer', a Jewish tinker in turn-of-the-century Russia accused of the ritual murder of a Gentile child. Most of the story takes place in prison, but despite its setting, the novel examines issues important in contemporary American life: accusation, guilt, responsibility, isolation, prejudice, self-reliance and identity. Continuing his exploration of these issues in *The Tenants* (1971), Malamud returned to the present in New York City and focused on the relationship between a Jewish apartment owner and the black tenant who refuses to leave the condemned building. The atmosphere of enclosure and actual or potential violence are also characteristic of Bellow's work, as even the titles of his first two novels suggest: *Dangling Man* (1945) and *The Victim* (1947).

The work of these writers is not, however, without humour, although the humour is often ironic and even painful or bitter. Roth's early work, such as *Goodbye, Columbus* (1959), offers comic treatments of serious subjects (the family, love, sexuality, gender relations, class, Jewish identity), which the author often treats with outrageous irreverence. In his later fiction about Zuckerman, a novelist very like himself, and in his moving autobiographical writings, Roth's humour is secondary to his insightful reflections on his own experiences. In these works, Roth explores what it means to be a writer in a modern, urban world, what it means to be a man and a Jew, a son and a husband, an intellectual and a human being – in other words, what it means from his perspective to be both an insider and an outsider in America.

▶ Look at Sylvia Plath's poem 'The Applicant' (pages 88–89). Who is 'the applicant'? Look carefully at the details the speaker mentions as he asks questions and tries to sell 'the applicant' a 'living doll'. What does this poem reveal about what men expected from women in the post-war years? How do you respond when the speaker says, 'Come here, sweetie, out of the closet'? Why do you suppose the speaker calls the 'living doll' 'it' rather than 'she' or 'her'? What does this poem suggest about Plath's understanding of the marketplace and women's roles in post-war America?

The post-war period does not, of course, end in the 1960s, nor does contemporary writing begin, for example, with the advent of the women's movement during that decade. A writer's career, like Roth's, may span the second half of the century, while the cataclysm of the Second World War was of such significance throughout the world that it is truly possible to see all of the American writing after 1945 as 'post-war', as somehow a response both to the war itself and to the issues it raised and the changes it brought about. The turmoil of the 1960s, however, did cause significant shifts of focus in American life and literature. Writing of the post-war years offers evidence of an alienation that became especially intense during the period of protest against U.S. involvement in the war in Southeast Asia. Mass demonstrations, in which many writers participated, was one response. Other reactions were more private, but just as connected to public events and attitudes. If we can see contemporary literature as having its beginnings in the late 1960s, we can do so in part because of the truth in a slogan popular at the time. Thinking Americans during that tumultuous decade began to struggle consciously with the implications of the statement that 'the personal is political'.

Contemporary writing

- What challenges did writers face at the end of the century?
- How have they responded to current issues?
- Did they look forward or backward at the turn of the millennium?

Social protest

By the late 1960s, the civil rights movement had become both narrower and broader, having stirred the passions of the nation. Although black Americans were legally entitled to 'equal rights', oppressive attitudes and conventions were deeply embedded in the power structure. Many Americans began to examine the nature of 'the establishment' more critically, while others drew back in horror at the protesters and their widening agenda, coining another slogan characteristic of the era: 'America – love it or leave it!' The assassinations of President John F. Kennedy in 1963 and Martin Luther King and Robert Kennedy in 1968 disturbed the nation, drawing attention to the violence and anger often just beneath the surface of the country's material prosperity.

The civil rights movement splintered in a variety of interesting ways. Radical black leaders, such as Eldridge Cleaver and Malcolm X, began to feel that integration was not the solution and grew hostile towards white supporters and common goals. The career of Imamu Amiri Baraka (b. 1934) illustrates this change. Born LeRoi Jones, he composed his early verse from the point of view of an individual in personal distress. In 'An Agony. As Now.' (1964), he wrote, 'I am inside someone/ who hates me. I look/ out from his eyes.' By the late 1960s, however, he had come to see his struggle as a black man in white America in political terms. He took a Muslim name and his writing became concerned with social change and separatism. In 'Black Art' (1969), Baraka concluded:

> We want a black poem. And a
> Black World.
> Let all the world be a Black Poem,
> And Let All Black People Speak This Poem
> Silently
> or LOUD.

The author's use of capital letters here emphasises a growing awareness of black community and the role of literature and language in achieving political ends.

Many white men and women, through participation in the civil rights movement, also began to have a deeper understanding of the nature of power – who had it, how governments and individuals used it, who was exploited by it and who profited from it. Public outrage over American escalation of the war in Vietnam under the Johnson (1963–1969) and then the Nixon (1969–1974) administrations led to demonstrations on university campuses throughout the nation as well as to mass protest marches on Washington. Even as reflective and personal a poet as Robert Lowell was galvanised, as were many intellectuals with a range of different temperaments, to involve themselves and their art in what they saw as a moral as well as a political crisis. Breaking the conventional boundaries between the private and the public, many writers began to approach their work in new ways, even challenging **generic** distinctions among fiction, poetry, drama and non-fiction, especially the essay, autobiography and history. Norman Mailer demonstrated his engagement with the issues of the time both in his semi-fictional

Why Are We in Vietnam? (1967) and in his mostly autobiographical and historical book *The Armies of the Night* (1968), with its roots in the author's own experiences during an important peace march on Washington in 1967. The black writer Michael Harper (b. 1938) similarly mixes **genres** in his poem 'American History' (1970), about a white racist reprisal against civil rights demonstrations:

> Those four black girls blown up
> in that Alabama church
> remind me of five hundred
> middle passage blacks
> in a net, under water
> in Charleston harbor
> so *redcoats* wouldn't find them.
> Can't find what you can't see
> can you?

Here Harper parallels a recent event with an 18th century incident in which slaves coming into a South Carolina harbour were hidden (and probably drowned in the process) so that British soldiers would not find them. The work's title draws attention to 'American History' as a 'cover up', while the poem itself forces the reader to think about the continuities between past injustices and those of the present. Harper is both writing history here and challenging the official versions of events as chronicled in the history Americans might have learned at school.

The 1960s and early 1970s were characterised not only by racial tensions and social protest against the war in Vietnam. This was also a period of experimentation – with drugs, with appearance, with traditional limits and taboos of all sorts – and of the 'sexual revolution'. The phrase 'alternative lifestyle' came in during this time and signalled the different ways many young people were trying to construct their lives. Some chose to try to live communally, breaking the conventions of the typical nuclear family; for others, living an 'alternative lifestyle' meant 'coming out', confronting their own gay or lesbian sexuality. Use of drugs, many of them hallucinogens such as LSD, was common on university campuses, while 'the pill' liberated women (and men) from the fear and consequences of pregnancy, as did the legalising of abortion in many states during the 1970s. All of these issues had both political and personal implications, and for many writers the two became inextricably intertwined as public matters seemed to demand everyone's involvement, while even one's intimate sexual life took on political implications. Richard Nixon spoke repeatedly against the protests of these years, insisting that, despite what he saw in the streets and on television as a vocal minority, the government's policies had the support of 'the silent majority' of the American people. In the face of such rhetoric, few writers felt they could remain silent.

The women's movement

The feminist movement, known in the late 1960s as 'women's liberation', had its roots in an understanding of this intersection of the personal and the political. Just as the protests against the war in Southeast Asia stemmed from the civil rights movement, modern feminism also had its beginnings in the protest against the oppression and exploitation of black people. Women's participation in this movement had often been limited to traditional and subservient tasks, while the philosophical arguments for black – and human – rights clearly implied a rethinking of gender relations. In the 1960s, the same sort of 'consciousness raising' began to happen for women as it did for black Americans; just as many black people became aware of their exploitation and their rights, so did many women. In her novel *The Women's Room* (1977), Marilyn French (b. 1929) vividly describes the changes among a group of female friends as they moved from an unquestioning acceptance of traditional roles towards an independence that challenged the established patriarchal order. The difficult changes French's characters experience would not have been possible, however, without the support of the group and the larger liberation movement.

Sylvia Plath

A writer such as Sylvia Plath also addressed feminist issues in her work, but in the early 1960s she saw and presented the problems posed by gender as personal and individual. In 'Three Women' (March 1962), Plath explored the different experiences of three nameless women on a maternity ward. The 'First Voice' goes through the process of giving birth to a healthy baby boy; she welcomes him as a 'miracle' who transforms her identity into that of a mother: 'I am a river of milk. / I am a warm hill.' All she wants is for him 'To love me as I love him,/ And to marry what he wants and where he will.' The 'Second Voice' comes onto the ward because she is experiencing a miscarriage. Blaming herself, she feels empty and unnatural, and declares, 'I am dying ... I lose a dimension. /... I am found wanting.' As she recovers and comes to terms with her loss, she insists, 'I am myself again'; determined to conceive another child, she comforts herself with the statement, 'I am a wife'. The 'Third Voice' is a woman who has decided to give up her child for adoption. She justifies her actions on the grounds that 'I wasn't ready', but she, too, feels a tremendous sense of loss. She is angry with the male doctors who deliver her baby, seeing them as somehow vaguely responsible for her predicament. When she leaves the hospital, she confesses, 'I am a wound', and although she finally feels as 'young as ever', she remains confused. Her last words to the reader are 'What is it I miss?' This poignant, dramatic poem examines important psychological moments brought about by physical, bodily experiences, but Plath does not look at these women's reactions as other than individual; she does not, despite occasional hints in the poem, examine the larger social and cultural attitudes that influence these women's reactions and shape – perhaps even determine – their ideas about themselves, their identity and self worth. The three voices speak in separate, apparently arbitrarily intermingled sections (the first, the second, the third, then the second, then the first again, then the third and so on), but they do not address one another. In this poem, Plath's women are typically isolated and alone.

In her work there is, in fact, no sense of female or feminist community which might help her speakers to understand their anguish in other than personal terms. Many of her poems echo the feelings of pain and distress found, for example, in Baraka's early verse before he fully joined the militant black movement. In 'Lesbos' (1962), for instance, Plath offers us what seems to be an encounter between two women in which the speaker actively disassociates herself from her female neighbour. It begins, 'Viciousness in the kitchen!' While the speaker in the poem realises that her neighbour, whom she is evidently visiting, has cleared her mind 'of voices and history', that she has been shaped by 'Hollywood' and that she supports a pathetic husband by filling 'him with soul-stuff, like a pitcher', the speaker can only despise her. Plath writes:

> I do not speak.
> I am packing the hard potatoes like good clothes,
> I am packing the babies,
> I am packing the sick cats ...
> I say I may be back.
> You know what lies are for.
>
> Even in your Zen heaven we shan't meet.

As in 'Three Women', there are hints in this poem of deep connections between the characters – indeed, it is possible to see the two women in 'Lesbos' as two aspects of the speaker's self – but the poem's conclusion insists on separation. Plath killed herself at the age of 30, having written her best poems within months of her death. There were many reasons for her suicide, but the overwhelming isolation voiced by the female speakers in her late work surely suggests that Plath would have understood, had she lived, the emphasis on social critique and female community fostered by the feminist movement and portrayed in French's novel.

Autobiographical writing

Writers during the 1960s and 1970s felt a stronger sense of community than in earlier decades. While there had always been groups of writers simultaneously living in more or less the same place (New York or San Francisco, for instance) and while there had been loosely constructed literary 'schools' (such as the Beats), during these decades American writers were joined by a host of common causes. Many of them met and communicated regularly with one another, encouraging an exciting exchange of ideas as they reflected both on their individual experiences and on what it meant to be an American. For many authors, their own lives and politics also seemed to require a more personal, even 'confessional' writing. Plath's poetry reflects this tendency as it moves from early, impersonal, academic verse to more open forms and a freer expression of feeling, while Norman Mailer is at once the author of *Armies of the Night* and a character within the text, as are many of the people he knew, for instance Robert Lowell. Specific writers often figure as obvious influences and actual subjects in one another's work, and it is more than a shared historic period which provides a context for understanding their writing; an author may actually situate his or her work within the context of another writer's work. Anne Sexton (1928–1974), who also took her own life, offers a good example. In 'Sylvia's Death' (17 February 1963), she writes about her personal friendship with Plath, whom she came to know when both poets attended Robert Lowell's poetry seminars in Boston in the late 1950s. Sexton recalls their discussions of suicide ('the death .../ ... we talked of so often each time/ we downed three extra dry martinis'), and asks,

> Sylvia, Sylvia,
> where did you go
> after you wrote me
> from Devonshire
> about raising potatoes
> and keeping bees?

Echoing Plath's own poetic subjects and rhythms, Sexton concludes her poem by calling out to her friend: 'O tiny mother,/ you too!/ O funny duchess!/ O blond thing!' Referring to a specific letter from Plath in 1962, Sexton anchors her poem in actual, personal experience, and it is a voice indistinguishable from Sexton's own self that utters the final lament in words that explicitly contextualise this poem in terms of Plath's own verse. Thus we can hear in the last lines of 'Sylvia's Death' such lines as 'O sister, mother, wife' from Plath's poem 'Amnesiac' (21 October 1962) or 'O Europe! O ton of honey!' at the end of Plath's 'The Swarm' (7 October 1962) or 'Trepanned veteran,/ Dirty girl,/ Thumb stump', lines addressed to the speaker's accidentally sliced finger in Plath's 'Cut' (24 October 1962). The specificity of the dates accompanying these poems further insists on the connection between the poets' experiences and their written work, explicitly inviting the reader to see the authors' lives as an important context for understanding their art.

Adrienne Rich

The work of Adrienne Rich, an important writer whose career spans the second half of the century, reflects many of the same issues raised by Plath and Sexton. In the 1950s, her verse was admired for its traditional features, and she made a careful point not to use first-person speakers who were in any way her personal self. If 'I' appeared in her work at all, it was either vague or an assumed voice, usually that of a nameless male figure. While acknowledging the difficulty of maintaining a woman's traditional role, she was even capable of advocating female subservience in an early poem such as 'An Unsaid Word' (1951):

> She who has power to call her man
> From that estranged intensity
> Where his mind forages alone,
> Yet keeps her peace and leaves him free,
> And when his thoughts to her return
> Stands where he left her, still his own,
> Knows this the hardest thing to learn.

By the mid–1960s, however, Rich had begun to experiment with looser, more open poetry, using conversational language while turning away from conventional patterns of rhyme and meter and subject. She also began to use a more personal voice and to focus on the lives and work of women such as Emily Dickinson in '"I am in Danger – Sir –"' (1964), a poem whose title is a quotation from one of Dickinson's letters, or 'Planetarium' (1968), a poem that names the astronomer Caroline Herschel (1750–1848). 'Planetarium' includes lines that indicate Rich's understanding of Harper's political point in 'American History': 'What we see, we see/ and seeing is changing'.

Rich became politically active in the 1960s and 1970s, first in the civil rights movement and then in the women's liberation movement that followed. Combining poetry and prose, her own words and those of other people in 'The Burning of Paper Instead of Children' (1968), Rich examined issues as various as the war in Vietnam, Nazi book burning and the significance of literature and language itself. These 'public' issues, however, are not the only matters that concern her here. Matters readers might at first consider 'private' or personal also come into the poem. In Section 3, she quotes and comments on a passage by one of her students in a special university programme designed to improve inadequate writing skills:

> *People suffer highly in poverty and it takes dignity and intelligence to overcome this suffering. Some of the suffering are: a child did not had dinner last night: a child steal because he did not have money to buy it:*

to hear a mother say she do not have money to buy food for her children and to see a child without cloth it will make tears in your eyes.

(the fracture of order
the repair of speech
to overcome this suffering)

The poem concludes:

I am composing on the typewriter late at night. ... A language is a map of our failures. Frederick Douglass [a 19th-century black abolitionist] wrote an English purer than Milton's. People suffer highly in poverty. There are methods but we do not use them. Joan [of Arc], who could not read, spoke some peasant form of French. Some of the suffering are: it is hard to tell the truth; this is America; I cannot touch you now. In America we have only the present tense. I am in danger. You are in danger. The burning of a book arouses no sensation in me. I know it hurts to burn. There are flames of napalm in Catonsville, Maryland. I know it hurts to burn. The typewriter is overheated, my mouth is burning, I cannot touch you and this is the oppressor's language.

Rich's anguish here brings together many of the issues facing the American writer during the last third of the century. 'The Burning of Paper Instead of Children' forces us to think of the 'burning' questions that disturb Rich. What is the value of history – both the past itself and any record of it? What is the nature of power – other people's and our own? What can the individual do about important public and private issues and are the two really separate? What is the value of language and literature, of reading and writing?

Rich herself continues to struggle with these challenging questions in her later verse and in her non-fiction. In 'Twenty-One Love Poems' (1974–1976), she emphasises the intimate relationship of two women within the context of which these and other questions arise in her daily life. She also uses this daring sequence of poems to explore the difficulties of her own individual experiences and psychology – the very material that, as a young poet in the middle of the century, she had been taught to avoid. The titles of her collections of verse in the last two decades of the 20th century suggest her ongoing concerns as well as her engagement with American identity: *A Wild Patience Has Taken Me This Far* (1981), *Your Native Land, Your Life* (1986), *Time's Power* (1989), *An Atlas of the Difficult World* (1991), *Dark Fields of the Republic* (1996) and *Midnight Salvage* (1999).

▶ Reread the passages from Adrienne Rich's 'The Burning of Paper Instead of Children', then try to answer the questions that the commentary suggests the poet is posing. What other questions do you think the author is asking here? In what ways does this poem (and other material by Rich on pages 8 and 91–95) illustrate that 'the personal is political'?

Alice Walker

Prose writers as well as poets were influenced by the activism of the 1960s. Alice Walker's (b. 1944) novel *Meridian* (1976), with its roots in her involvement in the civil rights movement, and her later novel *The Color Purple* (1982), are both shaped by her awareness of injustice in America. Reflecting on the need for role models, Walker discussed the plight of the modern artist in an important essay, 'Saving the Life That Is Your Own' (1976). Focusing particularly on those artists who are outside the dominant cultural mainstream, who are, for example, black or female or Jewish or gay, she singled out the novelist Toni Morrison (b. 1931), one of her black female contemporaries. Morrison has declared that she has written the sort of books she wanted to read because, in a society in which accepted literature is often sexist, racist and in other ways irrelevant or offensive to many people, she felt she had to do double work, serving as her own model as she wrote.

This need for models led Walker to do research on black women writers, in the course of which she discovered the work of Zora Neale Hurston. It is in some measure thanks to Walker that Hurston's work is now back in print and both read and written about. Thinking about the historical context which she has consciously used to define herself as a writer who is at once American, black and female, Walker insisted in her 1979 essay 'Zora Neale Hurston' that artists, as witnesses for the future, have a duty to collect forgotten figures, to rescue them from historical neglect.

This sort of 'collecting' is part of what Walker does in *The Color Purple*, a novel in letters which chronicles the life of Celie, a poor, abused, southern black woman, who slowly and painfully becomes conscious of the nature of her oppression. In utter loneliness, Celie begins the book by addressing her letters to God. Married off to a man she despises so much that she refuses to write his name, calling him only 'Mr. -----', she gradually realises the power of men over women, and starts to address her letters to her absent sister Nettie. At a climactic moment, Shug, Mr. -----'s lover, explains to Celie that she has misunderstood God as a white man. Through her deep friendship with Shug, Celie finally comes to understand not only the dynamics of power within 20th century American society, but her own individual self worth. Her anger is the first step towards her empowerment as an independent, creative person. Walker also suggests that as a result of her 'liberation', Celie has the potential to see herself differently in relation to the world around her; she will, in fact, discover a new relation to nature.

In 'Saving the Life that Is Your Own'(1976), Walker listed in addition to Hurston a number of other creative people whom she saw as role models because they understood that their experience as ordinary human beings was valuable and in danger of being falsified, misinterpreted, or lost: Jean Toomer, Colette, Anais Nin, Tillie Olsen, Virginia Woolf and Vincent Van Gogh. In her essay 'Being Female, Black, and Free' (1980), Margaret Walker (b. 1915), author of *Jubilee* (1966), a novel about the American Civil War, also wrote about self-awareness, anger and role models as important elements in the process of becoming an American writer. She pointed out, 'I think it took the women's movement to call my attention to cases of overt discrimination that hark back to my WPA days'. She continued, 'I have come through the fires of hell because I am a black woman, because I am poor, because I live in America, and because I am determined to be both a creative writer and maintain my inner integrity and my instinctive need to be free.' Realising that she had to write despite 'the pressures of a sexist, racist, violent, and most materialist society', Margaret Walker insisted that 'A writer needs certain conditions in which to work and create art. She needs a piece of time; a peace of mind; a quiet place; and a private life.' (from *The Writer on Her Work*, ed. Janet Sternburg, 1980) Like Alice Walker, Margaret Walker paid tribute in her essay to a number of role models, among them Phillis Wheatley, Jane Austen, George Eliot, George Sand, Emily Dickinson, Colette, Amy Lowell, Carson McCullers, Karen Blixen and Bessie Head.

▶ Find out more about the lives of those people Alice Walker and Margaret Walker mention as models. Alice Walker felt that Colette was fortunate not to have been born in America: why do think she felt this? What do you think she meant when she indicated that Virginia Woolf has 'saved so many of us', meaning writers? Why do you suppose Alice Walker and Margaret Walker admire these individuals? In what ways do they offer a context for their own work and that of other American women writers?

Countercultural response

At the turn of the millennium, American writers have emphasised their society's materialism and growing dependence on technology as increasingly alienating. While nearly all authors today, especially younger ones, use computers in their work, American writers in the last decades of the 20th century grew more and more sceptical about the benefits of technology while many individuals, like the fictional Celie, struggled to recast their relation to nature. The phrase 'back to nature' may have its roots in the rejection of urban life first evident in the suburbs of the 1950s, but was coined in the following decade when 'hippies' advocated leaving the cities and forging a new life in the countryside. Their models were, of course, America's first settlers in the 17th century and the 'pioneers', those generations of Americans who, throughout the 18th and 19th centuries, moved westward into an ever-diminishing frontier. Similarly, 'natural foods' and the idea of returning to the land were popularised during the 1960s and 1970s, as was vegetarianism, although it was not until the 1980s and 1990s that this sort of diet, with all of the ideological baggage that goes with it, gained any substantial following in the United States.

Widespread interest in ecological issues is, in fact, a world-wide issue, and this is an important point: at the beginning of the 21st century, more and more American issues are also simultaneously international issues. For instance, 'the pill', widely prescribed in the 1960s and 1970s not only in America but throughout the world, has been seen in the 1980s and 1990s to have a number of physically dangerous 'side effects' – not the least being that it protects no one from the possibility of venereal disease. The discovery of penicillin during the Second World War had encouraged many people to stop thinking of venereal disease as a serious problem. With the advent of AIDS in the 1980s, however, the sexual freedom of the 1960s was no longer possible. Thus the last years of the century demonstrated the grave and often unforeseen consequences of even our most personal behaviour. In turn, the global implications of such concerns as peace, war, poverty and human rights, combined with America's growing economic influence over the last hundred years, have made impossible the nation's earlier tendencies towards Isolationism. At the same time that some Americans continue to argue against America's political and military involvement in the affairs of other nations, it has become increasingly clear that America cannot think of itself as separate from the rest of the world. At the beginning of the 21st century, conservative Americans tend to support the idea of the United States as a global arbitrator because of what they see as its moral superiority, while liberals tend to argue for an international responsibility based on ethical obligation.

► Examine the passage from John Irving's novel *A Prayer for Owen Meany* (pages 97–98). What has gone wrong with America according to Owen Meany? Which other American writers would agree with his assessment? Which American writers present a vision of America that would contradict the one Irving suggests here? In Irving's novel, Owen Meany is speaking about America in the early 1960s. Compare his speech with Frost's poem 'The Gift Outright' (page 86), which Frost read on the occasion of John F. Kennedy's inauguration in 1961. What might account for the differences between Frost's vision of America and Irving's, written in the late 1980s?

The exploration of difference

These themes – a new relation to nature as well as individual and national responsibility for issues at once personal and global – have been significant for many writers in the last decades of the 20th century. Another, related theme is the celebration of difference, the exploration of individuality. For example, Simon J. Ortiz (b. 1941) writes about his Indian heritage, about an identity that is both fractured and integrated with an American past, present and future. When asked why he writes, Ortiz responded, 'The only way to continue is to tell a story ... Your children will not survive unless you tell something about them – how they were born, how they came to this certain place, how they continued.' (Simon J. Ortiz, in the preface to *A Good Journey*, 1977). In 'Passing through Little Rock' (1977), a city torn by racial strife in the 1960s, Ortiz bears witness to America's efforts to destroy Native American identity, while insisting on the possibility of renewal present in the vast expanses of uncorrupted nature still extant in the United States:

> The old Indian ghosts –
> 'Quapaw'
> 'Waccamaw' –
> are just billboard words
> in this crummy town ...
>
> I just want to cross the next hill,
> through that clump of trees
> and come out the other side
> and see a clean river,
> the whole earth new
> and hear the noise it makes
> at birth.

Exploring the relation between the personal and the national, the black poet Rita Dove (b. 1952) offers a verse chronicle of her grandparents' lives in *Thomas and Beulah* (1986), linking her family's history with the social history of America between 1900 and 1960. Told from two separate points of view, this sequence of poems also insists on both individual and shared experience.

Another contemporary writer, Alberto Ríos (b. 1952), draws on his Latino heritage in poems which often recall oral tradition while engaging with a natural world both real and imagined. In 'Wet Camp' (1982), he writes, 'We have been here before, but we are lost.' In 'Advice to a First Cousin' (1985), Ríos recounts his grandmother's words:

> ... look out for the next scorpion you see,
> she says, and makes a big face to scare me ...
> the way you must look out for men
> who have not yet bruised you.

Lorna Dee Cervantes (b. 1954) similarly engages with her Chicano past in a poem such as 'Visions of México While at a Writing Symposium in Port Townsend, Washington' (1981). In the first section, 'México', she writes of her identification with and separation from her Mexican heritage:

> I don't want to pretend I know more
> and can speak all the names. I can't.
> My sense of this land can only ripple through my veins ...
> I come from a long line of eloquent illiterates
> whose history reveals what words don't say.
> Our anger is our way of speaking ...

In the poem's second section, 'Washington', Cervantes writes about her conflicting feelings towards the United States, where she was born and raised, a country which she depicts as frequently degrading Mexicans. She begins, 'I don't belong this far north.' Still, without the benefits of growing up in prosperous post-war America, she is aware that she might never have become a writer.

Like the Chinese-American novelists Maxine Hong Kingston (b. 1940) and Amy Tan (b. 1952), Cathy Song (b. 1955), an Asian-American poet born and brought up in Hawaii, reveals a vivid sense of place in her verse as well an awareness of her oriental past. In 'Lost Sister' (1983), she writes of the 'daughters' in China who 'never left home':

> To move freely was a luxury
> stolen from them at birth.
> Instead, they gathered patience,
> learning to walk in shoes
> the size of teacups ...
> But they travelled far in surviving ...

Song parallels these Chinese daughters with the 'lost sister' who fled to 'another shore'. She asserts that:

> In America,
> there are many roads
> and women can stride along with men.
>
> But in another wilderness
> the possibilities,
> the loneliness,
> can strangulate like jungle vines.

The Chinese immigrant is liberated from oppressive traditions, but finds herself cut off from her roots. Song addresses her directly in the poem's final stanza:

> You find you need China:
> Your one fragile identification,
> a jade link
> handcuffed to your wrist.
> You remember your mother
> who walked for centuries
> footless –
> and like her,
> you have left no footprints,
> but only because
> there is an ocean in between,
> the unremitting space of your rebellion.

Li-Young Lee (b. 1957) is another Asian-American who writes about the contradictions of life in the United States, contradictions which are at once personal, national, and universal. In a pair of poems in which he reflects on his father's death, Lee compares two meals. In 'Eating Alone', he writes:

> White rice steaming, almost done. Sweet green peas
> fried in onions. Shrimp braised in sesame
> oil and garlic. And my own loneliness.
> What more could I, a young man, want.

This traditional meal reflects Lee's Chinese heritage, suggesting an established identity in positive terms which contrast ironically with the young man's loneliness and with the flat statement, which we might have expected to be a question, in the poem's concluding line. In 'Eating Together', Lee again describes a delicious meal, including a 'trout/ seasoned with slivers of ginger':

> We shall eat it with rice for lunch,
> brothers, sister, my mother who will
> taste the sweetest meat of the head,
> holding it between her fingers
> deftly, the way my father did weeks ago. Then he lay down
> to sleep like a snow-covered road
> winding through pines older than him,
> without any travelers and lonely for no one.

The final image of the dead father suggests, in its delicate detail, an oriental print of a calm landscape. The speaker's discomforting loneliness in the first poem is replaced with a sense of ongoing community, as the family eats together, and with an acceptance of the solitude of death, which is, ironically but affirmatively, a natural experience and 'lonely for no one'.

▶ Compare and contrast Frost's 'The Gift Outright' (page 86) and the extracts from 'On the Pulse of Morning' (pages 99–100), a poem written by Maya Angelou (b. 1928) for Bill Clinton's inauguration in 1993. What similar and different ideas about America do you find in these two poems? Does it matter that one is by a white man and the other by a black woman? Which do you feel more accurately reflects the America of its time? Do these poems tell the truth? Which poem do you feel is better for the occasion which it commemorates, or are both equally appropriate?

Contradictions

America has often portrayed itself as a 'melting pot', a nation to which people of various backgrounds might come and be welcomed. Its idealisation of itself as a land of freedom and opportunity for all is represented in the words, written by the Jewish poet Emma Lazarus (1849–1887), and inscribed in 1903 on the pedestal of the Statue of Liberty in New York City Harbor. Addressing the 'old world', the statue commands:

> ... 'Give me your tired, your poor,
> Your huddled masses yearning to breathe free,
> The wretched refuse of your teeming shore.
> Send these, the homeless, tempest-tossed to me,
> I lift my lamp beside the golden door!'

In fact, as its history and literature bear out, America has often not welcomed (much less, in melting pot fashion, erased) differences of region, race, colour, creed, class or gender. Yet the nation's literature at the turn of the millennium has been generally not disillusioned but optimistic, reflecting writers' hopes that, in spite of the increased complexities of our time, Americans have developed a sensitivity to and an understanding of politics and technology and power. America's historical emphasis on keeping different sorts of people apart has resulted in literature which explores differences of all sorts, whose writers celebrate those differences and America's special multiplicity in a variety of ways. Such interests mark American writing in a distinctive manner, while simultaneously placing it on a footing with international literature, also concerned at century's turn with issues that cross the boundaries of nation and culture – as well as with issues peculiar to particular nations with their individual histories.

Assignments

1 Look at several texts which respond to the experience of the First World War. A number of 'war' poems are included in Part 3: Texts and extracts, but you may also wish to consider novels, such as F. Scott Fitzgerald's *The Great Gatsby* (1925), Ernest Hemingway's *The Sun Also Rises* (1926) or *A Farewell to Arms* (1929), or Hemingway's short stories, especially those initially collected in the volume *In Our Time* (1925). What was the impact of the Great War on these American writers? What effect did they feel this war had on Americans and American society? What effect did they feel the war had on modern values more generally?

2 Consider one or more works by American authors particularly interested in exploring the inner workings of the mind, for instance, a character's unconscious or semi-conscious processing of emotional and factual material. Among the modernist writers you might look at are H.D., Gertrude Stein, Sherwood Anderson, Ernest Hemingway and William Faulkner. How does a writer's 'experimental' approach help us to understand the characters in their work? What is gained by this intimate access to a character's inner self?

3 Four popular films of the 1930s are readily available on video: *King Kong* (1933), *The Wizard of Oz* (1939), *Citizen Kane* (1939) and *Gone With the Wind* (1939). The first two are at least partly 'fantasies'; the second two attempt to engage in different ways with American history. Try to see one or more of these films and consider the following questions:

- How is power portrayed in these movies? Who has it and how is it used?
- What are these films saying about the relationship between men and women? About class and race? About money?
- In what ways, directly and indirectly, do these movies reflect American life and attitudes during the Depression era?
- What subjects and themes do these films share with the literature of the period? Are they trying to do the same or different things?

4 Look at one or more American works which respond to the Second World War. You might consider Norman Mailer's *The Naked and the Dead* (1948), James Jones' *From Here to Eternity* (1951), Joseph Heller's *Catch 22* (1961), Ken Kesey's *One Flew Over the Cuckoo's Nest* (1962),

Thomas Pynchon's *Gravity's Rainbow* (1973), William Styron's *Sophie's Choice* (1979), or Marge Piercy's *Gone to Soldiers* (1987). How is the war portrayed and what is its impact on Americans? Does it make a difference if the author is male or female? In what ways is a work about the Second World War also a work about the period in which it was written?

5 Look at the work of one or more black writers. Among those you might consider are James Baldwin, Gwendolyn Brooks, Charles W. Chestnut, Rita Dove, Langston Hughes, Zora Neale Hurston, Audre Lorde, Jean Toomer, Alice Walker, Margaret Walker, Richard Wright. You may want to do some basic research on these authors' lives and careers before deciding which ones to focus on.

- What does their work reveal about attitudes towards black people in America at the time during which they wrote?
- Do they feel hopeful or pessimistic about racial issues in America?
- To what degree do they feel defined – by others or by themselves, positively and/or negatively – by race?

6 Look at one or more American works about the conflict in Vietnam. You might consider Norman Mailer's *The Armies of the Night* (1968), Bobbie Ann Mason's *In Country* (1985), Susan Fromberg Schaeffer's *Buffalo Afternoon* (1989), or John Irving's A *Prayer for Owen Meany* (1989). You might want to consider an American film about this war, such as *Coming Home* (1978), *Platoon* (1986) or *Jacob's Ladder* (1990). What view of the war and America's involvement in it does the work convey? What moral dilemmas does it present? What do these works tell us about the experience of Vietnam and the nation's struggle to come to terms with it?

You might want to compare a work about the war in Vietnam with one about the Second or even the First World War. What differences do you notice? What similarities? The American actor John Wayne starred in several films set during World War Two. To extend your thinking further, you might look at one or more of these. How are such films different from literary representations of Americans during war? What accounts for these differences? You might think about differences in audience and when the films were made as opposed to when the novels were written.

7 Look at work by one or more women writers. You might consider such authors as Ann Beattie, Olga Broumas, Rita Dove, Marilyn French, Zora Neale Hurston, Audre Lorde, Marge Piercy, Sylvia Plath, Adrienne Rich, Anne Sexton, Cathy Song, Alice Walker, Margaret Walker. In deciding whom to focus on, you may first want to find out something about these authors' work and lives by doing a bit of basic research. Consider these questions:

- What kinds of relationships are these authors interested in exploring?
- What sort of relationships do the women in their work have with men?
- What sort of relationships do these female characters or speakers have with other women?
- What are these writers saying about gender and sexuality?
- What are they saying about the social forces in America that influence who we are?

8 In the final decades of the century, a number of writers have examined explicitly what it has meant and means to be gay. You might look at the work of such authors as Edmund White (b. 1940), Paul Monette (1945–1995), Mark Merlis (b. 1951), or David Leavitt (b. 1961). What sorts of attitudes and values made it particularly difficult to 'come out' in America? What has changed to make it possible for these authors to write about such experience? What American traditions can gay men affirm? What sorts of things do they protest against?

9 Compare and contrast two or more works by Asian-American writers. You might consider, for instance, Maxine Hong Kingston's *Woman Warrior* (1976) and Amy Tan's *The Joy Luck Club* (1989). What is the nature of the American experience for the characters in these novels? What are these authors saying about the particular period of American life covered in their work?

10 Look at one or more works of literature that engage with the subject of modern technology (there are several in Part 3: Texts and extracts). What problems does technology solve for these writers? What problems does it pose? Are technological achievements positive or negative? In what ways does technology in these works define, represent, limit or extend the possibilities of American experience?

2 Approaching the texts

Part 2 of *American Prose and Poetry in the 20th Century* examines the challenge of thinking and writing about 20th century American literature within a variety of contexts. It offers a number of examples for contextual reading as well as questions suitable for discussion and individual writing.

- How do I choose what to write about?
- How do I place American texts in context?
- Which context is the most appropriate one to develop?

Placing American literature in context

20th century American literature offers the reader a vast range of material. American writers have expressed themselves in a wide variety of ways and have often broken generic boundaries to create works that mix a number of genres. Readers need to ask not 'How does this work fit into a conventional form?' but 'How does this work challenge convention? Does it combine a number of forms or genres or traditions? In what ways do authors encourage us to read their work within particular contexts?' In responding to such questions, the reader needs to:

- look carefully at a writer's use of language, at the voice in the work, its tone and point of view
- think about the subject of the work, its characters, setting, and plot
- examine the work's ideas, the writer's attitudes, values and themes.

Some authors use more traditional forms, while others seek innovation. Some literary movements and periods, such as modernism in the 1920s, have encouraged writers to experiment with form as well as subject. Reading works as in part a response to the literary movements of their era is one way of reading 'in context'. For instance, we might read William Carlos Williams' 'The Red Wheelbarrow' (page 85) and ask ourselves in what ways this is a modernist poem. It would help to find out more about modernism in answering such a question, and in doing so, we would be enriching the context of our reading of this author's other works. Similarly, we might look at Allen Ginsberg's 'Howl' (pages 46–47) and 'A Supermarket in California (pages 87–88) as examples of 'Beat' poetry.

Any good piece of writing should be able to stand on its own, of course. A first reading often involves considering the work 'out of context': we may know little about the author, for instance, or even when or where it was written. Even so, we quickly come to the issue of context when, for example, we find an unfamiliar word or an allusion to an historical event or geography with which we are unfamiliar. Then we need to do some homework. We may want look up a strange or unusual word, paying particular attention to what it meant in America during the author's lifetime. We may need to find out more about a specific historical incident or period – the American Civil War or the peace protests of the 1960s, for instance. We may in some cases want to look closely at a map of the United States.

Biography

Sometimes we may want or even need to find out about an author's life, for it is not only the general history of the time which provides a context for reading but often the author's own particular experiences which can enrich our understanding of a literary work. Biography can be especially useful for approaching a writer such as Sylvia Plath, who frequently writes 'confessional' poetry, drawing explicitly on her own experiences. Other authors may write autobiographically, inviting us to look closely at the life that produced the work. Ernest Hemingway's *A Moveable Feast* (1964) is a carefully shaped, highly impressionistic account of his experiences in Paris forty years earlier. An awareness of Hemingway's own life can help us to understand the reality behind this book and the creative process which produced it. Some authors, such as Adrienne Rich and Alice Walker, have spoken and written about their own lives and their writing, offering us particular contexts for their work. Rich draws attention to her experiences as a lesbian, a Jew and a feminist writer in her poetry, while Walker emphasises her struggle as a black woman.

When reading a writer's life as the context for the work, however, we need to guard against seeing the written work as merely a window on the author's life. No matter how interesting a writer's life may be, it is the work that endures and should be the focus of our interest in any artist. Additionally, we need to be careful not to use biographical or even broad historical evidence to 'explain' the work; biography should enrich our understanding of a text, not reduce it to merely a piece of data.

Contexts suggested by the author

Authors often suggest, directly or indirectly, other contexts for reading their writing, for example through a dedication – as in Adrienne Rich's 'For Ethel Rosenberg' (pages 92–95) – or through an allusion; we may want to know what the Vietnam Memorial in Washington, D.C., looks like, for instance, when reading George Bilgere's 'At the Vietnam Memorial' (page 101).

Another common context for a literary text is another literary text. Thus, for instance, Fitzgerald evokes Keats' 'Ode to a Nightingale' by using a phrase from this poem as his title in *Tender Is the Night*. A detailed consideration of Keats' ode offers important insights into Fitzgerald's novel. Similarly, Ezra Pound surely expects us to bring an understanding of Walt Whitman to his poem 'A Pact' (page 80) and, by implication, to all of his mature verse.

Literary criticism

We can also think of literary criticism – either by the authors themselves, by their contemporaries, by earlier or later writers, or by scholars – as yet another context for literary works. For instance, Wordsworth's famous statement that 'poetry is emotion recollected in tranquillity' may help us to understand what he was trying to achieve, and also what he hoped his fellow English Romantic poets at the beginning of the 19th century were, or should have been, attempting.

▶ Is Wordsworth's famous statement useful in helping us to understand the extract from Baraka's poem 'Black Art' on page 51? How appropriate is the statement in understanding Adrienne Rich's 'Aunt Jennifer's Tigers' on page 91, or the extracts from 'The Burning of Paper Instead of Children' on pages 56–57?

Our own context

Another context which we inevitably bring to our reading, though we may not be entirely conscious of it, is the context of our own lives and times. In today's relatively permissive atmosphere, we may not be shocked by the innovations in rhyme and meter and orthography in e.e. cummings' 'in Just–' (page 24) or by his use of 's.' in 'i sing of Olaf glad and big' (pages 27–28). It is important, however, for us to be aware that most of his contemporary readers were quite surprised by these innovations and found cummings' poems amazingly experimental – although many other modernist artists in his circle saw his innovations merely as his way of doing what they were all doing in different ways. We should also be aware that we care about and respond especially deeply to literature which speaks to our own experiences and feelings. For instance, anyone uncomfortable with feminism might at first find Rich's work difficult or even wrong-headed. Similarly, anyone holding racist beliefs might find Margaret Walker's anger hard to take. If we have visited Paris or recall any time in the past when we were once very happy, we may be particularly moved by the extract from Hemingway's *A Moveable Feast* (pages 89–90).

The writer's work as a context

Perhaps the most important context for a particular text by a particular writer, however, is the rest of that writer's work. Thus the extracts included in Part 3 are best understood within the context of the works from which they are taken, although in this book they are offered primarily as contexts for other works. Authors in this volume are sometimes represented by several poems or extracts because these other texts provide a context, a **gloss**, a sort of commentary on the rest of their work. Sometimes this resonance is clearly encouraged by the author, as in the case of Li-Young Lee's two companion poems on page 63. At other times, early, middle and late work will illustrate interesting changes as well as continuities over the course of a writer's career. Work written at about the same time may show, through repetition, the depth of an author's convictions or, in contrast, different or conflicting moods or attitudes. With this in mind, you might compare several poems by Robert Frost (pages 85–86) or, rather than relying on someone else's selection, you might read independently an entire collection of poems by one author.

Assignments

1 For some writers, the reading of biography is an especially useful way to develop the context of our understanding. Find out more about the lives of one (or more) of the following authors: Angelou, Fitzgerald, Frost, Hemingway, Plath, Pound, Rich, Alice Walker. You might begin by consulting *Contemporary Authors* on CD-ROM.

What elements of these authors' lives enrich our reading of, for instance, a particular poem or short story? Specifically, how does our understanding of Hemingway's friendship with Fitzgerald help us to understand Hemingway's work? How does Plath's marriage to Ted Hughes provide information useful for understanding her poetry? How has Walker's work been influenced by her involvement in the civil rights movement and her efforts on behalf of what she would call not feminism but 'womanism'?

2 Several American artists have struggled to come to terms with the present by reworking – sometimes very freely – earlier literary texts. For instance, in his movie *Apocalypse Now* (1979), the American film maker Francis Ford Coppola 'rewrote' the English author Joseph Conrad's novel *Heart of Darkness* (1902). Paul Auster can be said to 'rewrite' Herman Melville's *Moby Dick* in his novel *Leviathan*. Consider one of these 'revisions': what is gained by changing the original context? Why do you suppose the author or film maker chose to contextualise his work specifically in terms of this particular earlier novel?

3 Texts and extracts

The texts and extracts that follow have been chosen to illustrate key themes and points made elsewhere in the book, and to provide material which may be useful when working on the assignments. The items are arranged chronologically.

Arthur Barlowe

From 'The First Voyage Made to the Coasts of America' (1589)

> ... we viewed the land about us, being where we first landed very sandy and low towards the waterside, but so full of grapes as the very beating and surge of the sea overflowed them, of which we found such plenty as well there as in all places else, both on the sand and on the green soil on the hills, [and] in the plains as well [as] on every little shrub, as also climbing towards the top of the high cedars, [so] that I think in all the world the like abundance is not to be found, and myself having seen those parts of Europe that most abound, find such difference [here] as were incredible to be written....
>
> This island had many goodly woods full of deer, coneys, hares, and fowl, even in the midst of summer in incredible abundance. The woods are not such as you find in Bohemia, Moscovia, or Hercynia, barren and fruitless, but the highest and reddest cedars of the world, far bettering the cedars of the Azores, of the Indies, or Lebanon, [and] pines, cypress, sassafras, the lentisk, ... and many other [trees] of excellent smell and quality. We remained by the side of this island two whole days before we espied one small boat rowing towards us, having in it three persons. This boat came to the island side, ... and there two of the people remaining, the third came along the shore towards us, ... And after he had spoken of many things not understood by us, we brought him, [to] his own good liking, aboard the ships, and gave him a shirt, a hat, and some other things, and made him taste of our wine, and our meat, which he liked very well ...
>
> The next day there came unto us divers boats, and in one of them the King's brother, accompanied with forty or fifty men, very handsome and goodly people, and in their behaviour as mannerly and civil as any of Europe. His name was Granganimeo, and the King is called Wingina, the country Wingandacoa, and now by her Majesty, "Virginia." ...
>
> He sent us every day a brace or two or fat bucks, coneys, hares,

fish, the best of the world. He sent us divers roots, and fruits very excellent good, and of their country corn, which is very white, fair and well-tasted, and grows three times in five months: in May they sow, in July they reap; in June they sow, in August they reap; in July they sow, in September they reap. ... The soil is the most plentiful, sweet, fruitful and wholesome of all the world ...

We found the people most gentle, loving, and faithful, void of all guile and treason, and such as live after the manner of the golden age. The people only care how to defend themselves from the cold in their short winter, and to feed themselves ...

Walt Whitman

From 'Song of Myself' (1855); 'Native Moments' (1860)

[Section 16]

I am of old and young, of the foolish as much as the wise,
Regardless of others, ever regardful of others,
Maternal as well as paternal, a child as well as a man,
Stuffed with the stuff that is coarse, and stuffed with the stuff that is fine,
One of the great nations, the nation of many nations – the smallest the same and the largest the same,
A southerner soon as a northerner, a planter nonchalant and hospitable,
A Yankee bound my own way.... ready for trade.... my joints the limberest joints on earth and the sternest joints on earth,
A Kentuckian walking the vale of the Elkhorn in my deerskin leggings,
A boatman over the lakes or bays or along the coasts.... a Hoosier, a Badger, a Buckeye,
A Louisianian or Georgian, a poke-easy from sandhills and pines,
At home on Canadian snowshoes or up in the bush, or with fisherman off Newfoundland,
At home in the fleet of iceboats, sailing with the rest and tacking,
At home on the hills of Vermont or in the woods of Maine or the Texan ranch,
Comrade of Californians.... comrade of free northwesterners, loving their big proportions,
Comrade of raftsmen and coalmen – comrade of all who shake hands and welcome to drink and meat;
A learner with the simplest, a teacher of the thoughtfulest,
A novice beginning experiment of myriads of seasons,
Of every hue and trade and rank, of every caste and religion,

Not merely of the New World but of Africa Europe or Asia....
a wandering savage,
A farmer, mechanic, or artist.... a gentleman, sailor, lover or quaker,
A prisoner, fancy-man, rowdy, lawyer, physician or priest,
I resist anything better than my own diversity,
And breathe the air and leave plenty after me,
And am not stuck up, and am in my place.
The moth and the fisheggs are in their place,
The suns I see and the suns I cannot see are in their place.
The palpable is in its place and the impalpable is in its place.

[Section 17]
These are the thoughts of all men in all ages and lands, they are not
original with me,
If they are not yours as much as mine they are nothing or next to
nothing,
If they do not enclose everything they are next to nothing,
If they are not the riddle and the untying of the riddle they are
nothing,
If they are not just as close as they are distant they are nothing.
This is the grass that grows wherever the land is and the water is,
This is the common air that bathes the globe.
This is the breath of laws and songs and behaviour,
This is the tasteless water of souls.... this is the true sustenance,
It is for the illiterate. ... it is for the judges of the supreme court. ...
it is for the federal capitol and the state capitols,
It is for the admirable communes of literary men and composers and
singers and lecturers and engineers and savans,
It is for the endless races of working people and farmers and seamen.

Native Moments
Native moments – when you come upon me – ah you are here now,
Give me now libidinous joys only,
Give me the drench of my passions, give me life coarse and rank,
To-day I go consort with Nature's darlings, to-night too,
I am for those who believe in loose delights, I share the midnight
orgies of young men,
I dance with the dancers and drink with the drinkers,
The echoes ring with our indecent calls, I pick out some low person
for my dearest friend,
He shall be lawless, rude, illiterate, he shall be one condemn'd by
others for deeds done,
I will play a part no longer, why should I exile myself form my
companions?

O you shunn'd persons, I at least do not shun you,
I come forthwith in your midst, I will be your poet,
I will be more to you than to any of the rest.

Charlotte Perkins Gilman

From 'The Yellow Wallpaper' (1892)

I don't know why I should write this.

I don't want to.

I don't feel able.

And I know John would think it absurd. But I must say what I feel and think in some way – it is such a relief!

But the effort is getting to be greater than the relief.

Half the time now I am awfully lazy, and lie down ever so much.

John says I mustn't lose my strength, and has me take cod liver oil and lots of tonics and things, to say nothing of ale and wine and rare meat.

Dear John! He loves me very dearly, and hates to have me sick. I tried to have a real earnest reasonable talk with him the other day, and tell him how I wish he would let me go and make a visit to Cousin Henry and Julia.

But he said I wasn't able to go, nor able to stand it after I got there; and I did not make out a very good case for myself, for I was crying before I had finished.

It is getting to be a great effort for me to think straight. Just this nervous weakness, I suppose.

And dear John gathered me up in his arms, and just carried me upstairs and laid me on the bed, and sat by me and read to me till it tired my head.

He said I was his darling and his comfort and all he had, and that I must take care of myself for his sake, and keep well.

He says no one but myself can help me out of it, that I must use my will and self-control and not let any silly fancies run away with me.

There's one comfort – the baby is well and happy, and does not have to occupy this nursery with the horrid wallpaper.

If we had not used it, that blessed child would have! What a fortunate escape! Why, I wouldn't have a child of mine, an impressionable little thing, live in such a room for worlds.

I never thought of it before, but it is lucky that John kept me here after all, I can stand it so much easier than a baby, you see.

Of course I never mention it to them any more – I am too wise – but I keep watch for it all the same.

There are things in that paper that nobody knows about but me, or ever will.

Behind that outside pattern the dim shapes get clearer every day.

It is always the same shape, only very numerous.

And it is like a woman stooping down and creeping about behind that pattern. I don't like it a bit. I wonder – I begin to think – I wish John would take me away from here!

Sarah Orne Jewett

From *The Country of the Pointed Firs* (1896)

... there was only one fault to find with this choice of a summer lodging-place, and that was its complete lack of seclusion. At first the tiny house of Mrs. Almira Todd, which stood with its end to the street, appeared to be retired and sheltered enough from the busy world, behind its bushy bit of a green garden, in which all the blooming things, two or three gay hollyhocks and some London-pride, were pushed back against the gray-shingled wall. It was a queer little garden and puzzling to a stranger, the flowers being put at a disadvantage by so much greenery; but the discovery was soon made that Mrs. Todd was an ardent lover of herbs, both wild and tame, and the sea-breezes blew into the low end-window of the house laden with not only sweet-brier and sweet-mary, but balm and sage and borage and mint, worm wood and southernwood. If Mrs. Todd had occasion to step into the far corner of her herb plot, she trod heavily upon thyme, and made its fragrant presence known with all the rest. Being a very large person, her full skirts brushed and bent almost every slender stalk that her feet missed. You could always tell when she was stepping about there, even when you were half awake in the morning, and learned to know, in the course of a few weeks' experience, in exactly which corner of the garden she might be.

At one side of this herb plot were other growths of a rustic pharmacopoeia, great treasures and rarities among the commoner herbs. There were some strange and pungent odors that roused a dim sense and remembrance of something in the forgotten past. Some of these might once have belonged to sacred and mystic rites, and have had some occult knowledge handed with them down the centuries; but now they pertained only to humble compounds brewed at intervals with molasses or vinegar or spirits in a small caldron on Mrs Todd's kitchen stove. They were dispensed to suffering neighbors, who usually came at night as if by stealth, bringing their own ancient-looking vials to be filled. ...

In taking an occasional wisdom-giving stroll in Mrs. Todd's company, and in acting as business partner during her frequent absences, I found the July days fly fast, and it was not until I felt myself confronted with too great pride and pleasure in the display, one night, of two dollars and twenty-seven cents which I had taken in during the day, that I remembered a long piece of writing, sadly belated now, which I was bound to do. ... Literary employments are so vexed with uncertianties at best, and it was not until the voice of conscience sounded louder in my ears than the sea on the nearest pebble beach that I said unkind words of withdrawal to Mrs. Todd. She only became more wistfully affectionate than ever in her expressions, and looked as disappointed as I expected when I frankly told her that I could no longer enjoy the pleasure of what we called "seein' folks".

Booker T. Washington

From *Up From Slavery* (1901)

To those of my race who depend on bettering their condition in a foreign land or who underestimate the importance of cultivating friendly relations with the Southern white man, who is their next-door neighbour, I would say: 'Cast down your bucket where you are' – cast it down in making friends in every manly way of the people of all races by whom we are surrounded. Cast it down in agriculture, mechanics, in commerce, in domestic service, and in the professions ...

Our greatest danger is that in the great leap from slavery to freedom we may overlook the fact that the masses of us are to live by the productions of our hands, and fail to keep in mind that we prosper in proportion as we learn to dignify and glorify common labour and put brains and skill into the common occupations of life; shall prosper in proportion as we learn to draw the line between the superficial and the substantial, the ornamental gewgaws of life and the useful. No race can prosper till it learns that there is as much dignity in tilling a field as in writing a poem. It is at the bottom of life we must begin, and not at the top. Nor should we permit our grievances to overshadow our opportunities.

To those of the white race who look to the incoming of those of foreign birth and strange tongue and habits for the prosperity of the South, were I permitted I would repeat what I say to my own race, 'Cast down your bucket where you are.' Cast it down among the eight millions of Negroes whose habits you know, whose fidelity and love

you have tested in days when to have proved treacherous meant the ruin of your firesides. Cast down your bucket among these people who have, without strikes and labour wars, tilled your fields, cleared your forests, builded your railroads and cities, and brought forth treasures from the bowels of the earth, and helped make possible this magnificent representation of the progress of the South. Casting down your bucket among my people, helping and encouraging them as you are doing on these grounds, and to education of head, hand, and heart, and you will find that they will buy your surplus land, make blossom the waste places in your fields, and run your factories. While doing this, you can be sure in the future, as in the past, that you and your families will be surrounded by the most patient, faithful, law-abiding, and unresentful people that the world has seen. As we have proved our loyalty to you in the past, in nursing your children, watching by the sick-bed of your mothers and fathers, and often following them with tear-dimmed eyes to their graves, so in the future, in our humble way, we shall stand by you with a devotion that no foreigner can approach, ready to lay down our lives, if need be, in defence of yours, interlacing our industrial, commercial, civil, and religious life with yours in a way that shall make the interests of both races one. In all things that are purely social we can be as separate as the fingers, yet one as the hand in all things essential to mutual progress ...

W.E.B. Du Bois

From *The Souls of Black Folk* (1903)

Mr Washington distinctly asks that black people give up, at least for the present, three things, –

First, political power,

Second, insistence on civil rights,

Third, higher education of Negro youth, -

and concentrate all their energies on industrial education, the accumulation of wealth, and the conciliation of the South. This policy has been courageously and insistently advocated for over fifteen years, and has been triumphant for perhaps ten years. As a result of this tender of the palm-branch, what has been the return? In these years there have occurred:

1 The disfranchisement of the Negro.

2 The legal creation of a distinct status of civil inferiority for the Negro.

3 The steady withdrawal of aid from institutions for the higher training of the Negro. ...

This triple paradox in Mr. Washington's position is the object of criticism by two classes of colored Americans. One class is spiritually descended from Toussaint the Saviour, through Gabriel, Vesey, and Turner, and they represented the attitude of revolt and revenge; they hate the white South blindly and distrust the white races generally, and so far as they agree on definite action, think that the Negro's hope lies in emigration beyond the borders of the United States. And yet, by the irony of fate, nothing has more effectually made this programme seem hopeless than the recent course of the United States toward weaker and darker peoples in the West Indies, Hawaii, and the Philippines – for where in the world may we go and be safe from lying and brute force? ...

The other class of Negroes who cannot agree with Mr. Washington has hitherto said little aloud. ... Such men feel in conscience bound to ask of this nation three things:

1 The right to vote.

2 Civic equality.

3 The education of youth according to ability. ...

So far as Mr. Washington preaches Thrift, Patience, and Industrial Training for the masses, we must hold up his hands and strive with him, rejoicing in his honors and glorying in the strength of this Joshua called of God and of man to lead the headless host. But so far as Mr. Washington apologizes for injustice, North or South, does not rightly value the privilege and duty of voting, belittles the emasculating effects of caste distinctions, and opposes the higher training and ambition of our brighter minds, – so far as he, the South, or the Nation, does this, – we must unceasingly and firmly oppose them. By every civilised and peaceful method we must strive for the rights which the world accords to men, clinging unwaveringly to those great words which the sons of the Fathers would fain forget: "We hold these truths to be self-evident: That all men are created equal; that they are endowed by their Creator with certain unalienable rights; that among these are life, liberty, and the pursuit of happiness."

Ezra Pound

'A Pact' (1913); 'In a Station of the Metro' (1913)

A Pact
I make a pact with you, Walt Whitman –
I have detested you long enough.
I come to you as a grown child
Who has had a pig-headed father;
I am old enough now to make friends.
It was you that broke the new wood,
Now is a time for carving.
We have one sap and one root –
Let there be commerce between us.

In a Station of the Metro
The apparition of these faces in the crowd;
Petals on a wet, black bough.

H.D. (Hilda Doolittle)

'Oread' (1914)

Oread
Whirl up, sea –
whirl your pointed pines,
splash your great pines
on our rocks,
hurl your green over us,
cover us with your pools of fir.

Carl Sandburg

'Fog' (1916); 'Salvage' (1916); 'Happiness' (1916)

Fog
The fog comes
on little cat feet.

It sits looking
over harbor and city
on silent haunches
and then moves on.

Salvage

Guns on the battle lines have pounded now a year between Brussels and Paris.

And, William Morris, when I read your old chapter on the great arches and naves and little whimsical corners of the Churches of Northern France – Brr-rr!

I'm glad you're a dead man, William Morris, I'm glad you're down in the damp and mouldy, only a memory instead of a living man – I'm glad you're gone.

You never lied to us, William Morris, you loved the shape of those stones piled and carved for you to dream over and wonder because workmen got joy of life into them,

Workmen in aprons singing while they hammered, and praying, and putting their songs and prayers into the walls and roofs, the bastions and cornerstones and gargoyles – all their children and kisses of women and wheat and roses growing.

I say, William Morris, I'm glad you're gone, I'm glad you're a dead man.

Guns on the battle lines have pounded a year now between Brussels and Paris.

Happiness

I asked professors who teach the meaning of life to tell me what is happiness.

And I went to famous executives who boss the work of thousands of men.

They all shook their heads and gave me a smile as though I was trying to fool with them.

And then one Sunday afternoon I wandered out along the Desplaines river.

And I saw a crowd of Hungarians under the trees with their women and children and a keg of beer and an accordion.

Sherwood Anderson

From *Winesburg, Ohio* (1919)

During the early fall of her twenty-seventh year a passionate restlessness took possession of Alice. She could not bear to be in the company of the drug clerk, and when, in the evening, he came to walk with her she sent him away. Her mind became intensely active and when, weary from the long hours of standing behind the counter in the store, she went home and crawled into bed, she could not sleep. With staring eyes she looked into the darkness. Her imagination, like a child awakened from long sleep, played about the room. Deep within her there was something that would not be cheated by phantasies and that demanded some definite answer from life.

Alice took a pillow into her arms and held it tightly against her breasts. Getting out of bed, she arranged a blanket so that in the darkness it looked like a form lying between the sheets and, kneeling beside the bed, she caressed it, whispering words over and over, like a refrain. "Why doesn't something happen? Why am I left here alone?" she muttered. Although she sometimes thought of Ned Currie, she no longer depended on him. Her desire had grown vague. She did not want Ned Currie or any other man. She wanted to be loved, to have something answer the call that was growing louder and louder within her.

And then one night when it rained Alice had an adventure. It frightened and confused her. She had come home from the store at nine and found the house empty. ... Alice went upstairs to her room and undressed in the darkness. For a moment she stood by the window hearing the rain beat against the glass and then a strange desire took possession of her. Without stopping to think of what she intended to do, she ran downstairs through the dark house and out into the rain. As she stood on the little grass plot before the house and felt the cold rain on her body a mad desire to run naked through the streets took possession of her.

She thought that the rain would have some creative and wonderful effect on her body. Not for years had she felt so full of youth and courage. She wanted to leap and run, to cry out, to find some other lonely human and embrace him. On the brick sidewalk before the house a man stumbled homeward. Alice started to run. A wild, desperate mood took possession of her. "What do I care who it is. He is alone, and I will go to him," she thought; and then without stopping to consider the possible result of her madness, called softly.

"Wait!" she cried. "Don't go away. Whoever you are, you must wait."

The man on the sidewalk stopped and stood listening. He was an old man and somewhat deaf. Putting his hand to his mouth, he shouted, "What? What say?" he called.

Alice dropped to the ground and lay trembling. She was so frightened at the thought of what she had done that when the man had gone on his way she did not dare get to her feet, but crawled on hands and knees through the grass to the house. When she got to her room she bolted the door and drew her dressing table across the doorway. Her body shook as with a chill and her hands trembled so that she had difficulty getting into her nightdress. When she got into bed she buried her face in the pillow and wept broken-heartedly. "What is the matter with me? I will do something dreadful if I am not careful," she thought, and turning her face to the wall, began trying to force herself to face bravely the fact that many people must live and die alone, even in Winesburg.

Sinclair Lewis

From *Babbitt* (1922)

The towers of Zenith aspired above the morning mist; austere towers of steel and cement and limestone, sturdy as cliffs and delicate as silver rods. They were neither citadels nor churches, but frankly and beautifully office buildings.

The mist took pity on the fretted structures of earlier generations: the Post Office with its shingle-tortured mansard, the red brick minarets of hulking old houses, factories with stingy and sooted windows, wooden tenements coloured like mud. The city was full of such grotesqueries, but the clean towers were thrusting them from the business centre, and on the farther hills were shining new houses, homes – they seemed – for laughter and tranquillity.

Over a concrete bridge fled a limousine of long sleek hood and noiseless engine. These people in evening clothes were returning from an all-night rehearsal of a Little Theatre play, an artistic adventure considerably illuminated by champagne. Below the bridge curved a railway, a maze of green and crimson lights. The New York Flyer boomed past, and twenty lines of polished steel leaped into the glare.

In one of the skyscrapers the wires of the Associated Press were being closed. The telegraph operators wearily raised their celluloid eye-shades after a night of talking with Paris and Peking. Through the building crawled the charwomen, yawning, their old shoes slapping. The dawn mist spun away. Queues of men with lunch-boxes clumped toward the immensity of new factories, sheets of glass and hollow tile, glittering shops where five thousand men worked beneath one roof, pouring out the honest wares that would be sold up the Euphrates and across the veldt. The whistles rolled out in greeting a chorus cheerful as the April dawn; the song of labor in a city built – it seemed – for giants.

* * * * * * * * *

There was nothing of the giant in the aspect of the man who was beginning to awaken in the sleeping-porch of a Dutch Colonial house in that residential district of Zenith known as Floral Heights.

His name was George F. Babbitt. He was forty-six years old now, in April, 1920, and he made nothing in particular, neither butter nor shoes nor poetry, but he was nimble in the calling of selling houses for more than people could afford to pay.

His large head was pink, his brown hair thin and dry. His face was babyish in slumber, despite his wrinkles and the red spectacle-dents on the slopes of his nose. He was not fat but he was exceedingly well fed; his cheeks were pads, and the unroughened hand which lay helpless upon the khaki-veloured blanket was slightly puffy. He seemed prosperous, extremely married and unromantic; and altogether unromantic appeared this sleeping-porch, which looked on one sizable elm, two respectable grass-plots, a cement drive, and a corrugated iron garage. Yet Babbitt was again dreaming of the fairy child, a dream more romantic than scarlet pagodas by a silver sea.

For years the fairy child had come to him. When others saw but Georgie Babbitt, she discerned gallant youth. She waited for him, in the darkness beyond mysterious groves. When at last he could slip away from the crowded house he darted to her. His wife, his clamouring friends, sought to follow, but he escaped, the girl fleet beside him, and they crouched together on a shadowy hillside. ...

Babbitt moaned, turned over, struggled back toward his dream. ... He glanced once at his favourite tree, elm twigs against the gold patina sky, and fumbled for sleep as for a drug. He who had been a boy very credulous of life was no longer greatly interested in the possible and improbable adventures of each new day.

* * * * * * * * *

If you had asked Babbitt what his religion was, he would have answered in sonorous Boosters'–Club rhetoric, "My religion is to serve my fellow men, to honour my brother as myself, and to do my bit to make life happier for one and all." If you had pressed him for more detail, he would have announced, "I'm a member of the Presbyterian Church, and naturally, I accept its doctrines." If you had been so brutal as to go on, he would have protested, "There's no use discussing and arguing about religion; it just stirs up bad feeling."

Actually, the content of his theology was that there was a supreme being who had tried to make us perfect, but presumably had failed; that if one was a Good Man he would go to a place called Heaven (Babbitt unconsciously pictured it as rather like an excellent hotel with a private garden), but if one was a Bad Man, that is, if he murdered or committed burglary or used cocaine or had mistresses, or sold non-existent real estate, he would be punished. Babbitt was uncertain, however, about what he called "this business of Hell." ...

Upon this theology he rarely pondered. The kernel of his practical religion was that it was respectable, and beneficial to one's business, to be seen going to services; that the church kept the Worst Elements from being still worse; and that the pastor's sermons, however dull they might seem at the time of taking, yet had a voodooistic power which "did a fellow good – kept him in touch with Higher Things."

William Carlos Williams

'The Red Wheelbarrow' (1923)

The Red Wheelbarrow
so much depends
upon

a red wheel
barrow

glazed with rain
water

beside the white
chickens

Robert Frost

'Fire and Ice' (1923); 'The Secret Sits' (1936); 'Desert Places' (1936); 'The Gift Outright' (1942)

Fire and Ice
Some say the world will end in fire,
Some say in ice.
From what I've tasted of desire
I hold with those who favor fire.
But if it had to perish twice,
I think I know enough of hate
To say that for destruction ice
Is also great
And would suffice.

The Secret Sits

We dance round in a ring and suppose,
But the Secret sits in the middle and knows.

Desert Places

Snow falling and night falling fast, oh, fast
In a field I looked into going past,
And the ground almost covered smooth in snow,
But a few weeds and stubble showing last.

The woods around it have it – it is theirs.
All animals are smothered in their lairs.
I am too absent-spirited to count;
The loneliness includes me unawares.

And lonely as it is, that loneliness
Will be more lonely ere it will be less –
A blanker whiteness of benighted snow
With no expression, nothing to express.

They cannot scare me with their empty spaces
Between stars – on stars where no human race is.
I have it in me so much nearer home
To scare myself with my own desert places.

The Gift Outright

The land was ours before we were the land's.
She was our land more than a hundred years
Before we were her people. She was ours
In Massachusetts, in Virginia,
But we were England's, still colonials,
Possessing what we still were unpossessed by,
Possessed by what we now no more possessed.
Something we were withholding made us weak
Until we found out that it was ourselves
We were withholding from our land of living,
And forthwith found salvation in surrender.
Such as we were we gave ourselves outright
(The deed of gift was many deeds of war)
To the land vaguely realizing westward,
But still unstoried, artless, unenhanced,
Such as she was, such as she would become.

Wallace Stevens

'The Death of a Soldier' (1931)

The Death of a Soldier

Life contracts and death is expected,
As in a season of autumn.
The soldier falls.

He does not become a three-days personage,
Imposing his separation,
Calling for pomp.

Death is absolute and without memorial,
As in a season of autumn,
When the wind stops,

When the wind stops and, over the heavens,
The clouds go, nevertheless,
In their direction.

Allen Ginsberg

'A Supermarket in California' (Berkeley, California, 1955)

A Supermarket in California

What thoughts I have of you tonight, Walt Whitman, for I walked down the sidestreets under the trees with a headache self-conscious looking at the full moon.

In my hungry fatigue, and shopping for images, I went into the neon fruit supermarket, dreaming of your enumerations!

What peaches and what penumbras! Whole families shopping at night! Aisles full of husbands! Wives in the avocados, babies in the tomatoes! – and you, Garcia Lorca, what were you doing down by the watermelons?

I saw you, Walt Whitman, childless, lonely old grubber, poking among the meats in the refrigerator and eyeing the grocery boys.

I heard you asking questions of each: Who killed the pork chops? What price bananas? Are you my Angel?

I wandered in and out of the brilliant stacks of cans following you, and followed in my imagination by the store detective.

We strode down the open corridors together in our solitary fancy tasting artichokes, possessing every frozen delicacy, and never passing the cashier.

Where are we going, Walt Whitman? The doors close in an hour. Which way does your breard point tonight?

(I touch your book and dream of our odyssey in the supermarket and feel absurd.)

Will we walk all night through solitary streets? The trees add shade to shade, lights out in houses, we'll both be lonely.

Will we stroll dreaming of the lost America of love past blue automobiles in driveways, home to our silent cottage?

Ah, dear father, graybeard, lonely old courage-teacher, what America did you have when Charon quit poling his ferry and you got out on a smoking bank and stood watching the boat disappear on the black waters of Lethe?

Sylvia Plath

'The Applicant' (11 October 1962)

The Applicant

First, are you our sort of a person?
Do you wear
A glass eye, false teeth or a crutch,
A brace or a hook,
Rubber breasts or a rubber crotch,

Stitches to show something's missing? No, no? Then
How can we give you a thing?
Stop crying.
Open your hand.
Empty? Empty. Here is a hand

To fill it and willing
To bring teacups and roll away headaches
And do whatever you tell it.
Will you marry it?
It is guaranteed

To thumb shut your eyes at the end
And dissolve of sorrow.
We make new stock from the salt.
I notice you are stark naked.
How about this suit –

Black and stiff, but not a bad fit.
Will you marry it?
It is waterproof, shatterproof, proof
Against fire and bombs through the roof.
Believe me, they'll bury you in it.

Now your head, excuse me, is empty.
I have the ticket for that.
Come here, sweetie, out of the closet.
Well, what do you think of *that*?
Naked as paper to start

But in twenty-five years she'll be silver,
In fifty, gold.
A living doll, everywhere you look.
It can sew, it can cook,
It can talk, talk, talk.

It works, there is nothing wrong with it.
You have a hole, it's a poultice.
You have an eye, it's an image.
My boy, it's your last resort.
Will you marry it, marry it, marry it.

Ernest Hemingway

From *A Moveable Feast* (1964)

Then, instead of the two of them and their child, there are three of them. First it is stimulating and fun and it goes on that way for a while. All things truly wicked start from an innocence. So you live day by day and enjoy what you have and do not worry. You lie and hate it and it destroys you and every day is more dangerous, but you live day to day as in a war.

It was necessary that I have leave Schruns and go to New York to rearrange publishers. I did my business in New York and when I got back to Paris I should have caught the first train from the Gare de l'Est that would take me down to Austria. But the girl I was in love with was in Paris then, and I did not take the first train, or the second or the third.

When I saw my wife again standing by the tracks as the train came in by the piled logs at the station, I wished I had died before I ever loved anyone but her. She was smiling, the sun on her lovely face tanned by the snow and sun, beautifully built, her hair red gold in the sun, grown out all winter awkwardly and beautifully, and Mr. Bumpy standing with her, blond and chunky and with winter cheeks looking like a good Vorarlberg boy.

"Oh, Tatie," she said, when I was holding her in my arms, "you're back and you made such a fine successful trip. I love you and we've missed you so."

I loved her and I loved no one else and we had a lovely magic time while we were alone. I worked well and we made great trips, and I thought we were invulnerable again, and it wasn't until we were out of the mountains in late spring, and back in Paris that the other thing started again.

That was the end of the first part of Paris. Paris was never to be the same again although it was always Paris and you changed as it changed. We never went back to the Vorarlberg and neither did the rich.

There is never any ending to Paris and the memory of each person who has lived in it differs from that of any other. We always returned to it no matter who we were or how it was changed or with what difficulties, or ease, it could be reached. Paris was always worth it and you received return for whatever you brought to it. But this is how Paris was in the early days when we were very poor and very happy.

Lucille Clifton

'Richard Penniman' (1972)

Richard Penniman
when his Mama and Daddy died
put on an apron and long pants
and raised up twelve brothers and sisters.
When a whitey asked one of his brothers one time
is Little Richard a man (or what?)
he replied in perfect understanding
you bet your faggot ass
he is
you bet your dying ass.

Adrienne Rich

'Aunt Jennifer's Tigers' (1951); from 'Twenty-One Love Poems' (1974–1976); 'For Ethel Rosenburg' (1980)

Aunt Jennifer's Tigers

Aunt Jennifer's tigers prance across a screen,
Bright topaz denizens of a world of green.
They do not fear the men beneath the tree;
They pace in sleek chivalric certainty.

Aunt Jennifer's fingers fluttering through her wool
Find even the ivory needle hard to pull.
The massive weight of Uncle's wedding band
Sits heavily upon Aunt Jennifer's hand.

When Aunt is dead, her terrified hands will lie
Still ringed with ordeals she was mastered by.
The tigers in the panel that she made
Will go on prancing, proud and unafraid.

From 'Twenty-One Love Poems'

XII

Sleeping, turning in turn like planets
rotating in their midnight meadow:
a touch is enough to let us know
we're not alone in the universe, even in sleep:
the dream-ghosts of two worlds
walking their ghost-towns, almost address each other.
I've wakened to your muttered words
spoken light– or dark-years away
as if my own voice had spoken.
But we have different voices, even in sleep,
and our bodies, so alike, are yet so different
and the past echoing through our bloodstreams
is freighted with different language, different meanings -
though in any chronicle of the world we share
it could be written with new meaning
we were two lovers of one gender,
we were two women of one generation.

For Ethel Rosenburg

Convicted, with her husband, of "conspiracy to commit espionage"; killed in the electric chair June 19, 1953

1

Europe 1953:
throughout my random sleepwalk
the words

scratched on walls, on pavements
painted over railway arches
Liberez les Rosenberg!

Escaping from home I found
home everywhere:
the Jewish question, Communism

marriage itself
a question of loyalty
or punishment

my Jewish father writing me
letters of seventeen pages
finely inscribed harangues

questions of loyalty
and punishment
One week before my wedding

that couple gets the chair
the volts grapple her, don't
kill her fast enough

Liberez les Rosenberg!
I hadn't realized
our family arguments were so important

my narrow understanding
of crime of punishment
no language for this torment

mystery of that marriage
always both faces
on every front page in the world

Something so shocking   so
unfathomable
it must be pushed aside

2

She sank however into my soul   A weight of sadness
I hardly can register how deep
her memory has sunk   that wife and mother

like so many
who seemed to get nothing out of any of it
except her children

that daughter   of a family
like so many
needing its female monster

she, actually wishing to be   *an artist*
wanting out of poverty
possibly also really wanting
revolution

that woman   strapped in the chair
no fear and no regrets
charged by prosperity

not with selling secrets to the Communists
but with wanting   *to distinguish*
herself   being a bad daughter   a bad mother

And I   walking to my wedding
by the same token a bad daughter   a bad sister
my forces focused

on that hardly revolutionary effort
Her life and death   the possible
ranges of disloyalty

so painful   so unfathomable
they must be pushed aside
ignored for years

3

Her mother testifies against her
Her brother testifies against her
After her death

she becomes a natural prey for pornographers
her death itself a scene
her body *sizzling   half-strapped   whipped like a sail*

She becomes the extremist victim
described nonetheless as *rigid of will*
what are her politics by then   no one knows

Her figure sinks into my soul
a drowned statue
sealed in lead

For years it has lain there   unabsorbed
first as part of that dead couple
on the front pages of the world   the week

I gave myself in marriage
then slowly severing   drifting apart
a separate death   a life unto itself

no longer *the Rosenburgs*
no longer the chosen scapegoat
the family monster

till I hear how she sang
a prostitute to sleep
in the Women's House of Detention

Ethel Greenglass Rosenburg   would you
have marched to take back the night *
collected signatures

for battered women who kill
What would you have to tell us
would you have burst the net

*To make the night safe, to free women from the threat of sexual and other violence

4

Why do I even want to call her up
to console my pain   (she feels no pain at all)
why do I wish to put such questions

to ease myself   (she feels no pain at all
she   finally burned to death   like so many)
why all this exercise of hindsight?

since   if I imagine her at all
I have to imagine first
the pain inflicted on her   by women

her mother testifies against her
her sister-in-law testifies against her
and how she sees it

not the impersonal forces
not the historical reasons
why they might have hated her strength

If I have held her at arm's length till now
if I have still believed it was
my loyalty, my punishment at stake

if I dare imagine her surviving
I must be fair to what she must have lived through
I must allow her to be at last

political in her ways   not in mine
her urgencies perhaps   impervious to mine
defining revolution as she defines it

or, bored to the marrow of her bones
with "politics"
bored with the vast boredom of long pain

small; tiny in fact; in her late sixties
liking her room   her private life
living alone perhaps

no one you could interview
maybe filling a notebook herself
with secrets she has never sold

E. L. Doctorow

From *World's Fair* (1985)

This is an essay I sent to the World's Fair on the theme of the Typical American Boy.

> *The typical American Boy is not fearful of Dangers. He should be able to go out into the country and drink raw milk. Likewise, he should traverse the hills and valleys of the city. If he is Jewish he should say so. If he is anything he should say what it is when challenged. He roots for his home team in football and baseball but also plays sports himself. He reads all the time. It's all right for him to like comic books so long as he knows they are junk. Also, radio programs and movies may be enjoyed but not at the expense of important things. For example he should always hate Hitler. In music he appreciates both swing and symphony. In women he appreciates them all. He does not waste time daydreaming when he is doing his homework. He is kind. He cooperates with his parents. He knows the value of a dollar. He looks death in the face.*

Once I had done it, I copied it out in my best penmanship. I had to copy it twice because just as I got to the end the first time my pen leaked and I got a big blot in the margin. I mailed it according to all the rules, and then I stopped thinking about it. I had given the American Boy contest everything I had, but now it was out of my hands and so I wanted it out of my mind as well. I knew these things took a very long time. Even when you sent away for something you had to allow six weeks delivery. I never understood why, but there it was. ...

'Our son entered a contest and won,' my father said.

I was peering over his shoulder at the news story. I was one of six honourable mentions. The winner was an eighth grader from P.S. 53.

'Not exactly,' I said. I was trying to appear casual about the whole thing, but there was my name in black and white in the newspaper. My mother had sat down on the couch. 'When did this happen?' she said. 'I knew nothing about a contest.'

'My name is in the newspaper!' I shouted. 'I'm famous! I'm in the newspaper!'

Then we were all laughing. I hugged my father. I ran across the room and hugged my mother. 'You're full of surprises, aren't you?' she said.

My father read the entire news story aloud. Included in the account was an excerpt from the winning essay. ' "The typical

American boy should possess the same qualities as those of the early American pioneers. He should be handy, dependable, courageous, and loyal to his beliefs. He should be clean, cheerful and friendly, willing to help and be kind to others. He is an all around boy interested in sports, hobbies, and the world around him. ... The typical American boy takes good care of public property he uses. He enjoys the comics, the movies, outdoor games, pets, and radio programs. He is usually busy at some handicraft or hobby and is always thinking up something new to do or make. That is why America still has a future."'

I folded my arms across my chest. 'It's not that good,' I said. 'It sounds like the Boy Scout pledge. A Scout should be courteous, friendly, clean and all that drivel.'

'Now, Edgar,' my mother said.

I was upset. I had had sports in mine too, and kindness. He had pioneers. Why hadn't I thought of that? And he had brought in the future of America. He was right – the typical American boy mentions America.

John Irving

From *A Prayer For Owen Meany* (1989)

'Did you hear about Marilyn Monroe?' he asked us again. Suddenly, it didn't sound like a joke. Maybe it's about the Kennedys! I thought.

'No. What about her?' I said.

'She's dead.' ...

'How?' I asked the ski bum.

'An overdose,' he said; he sounded disappointed – as if he'd been hoping for something bloodier. 'Maybe it was an accident, maybe it was suicide,' he said.

Maybe it was the Kennedys, I thought. It made me feel afraid; at first, that summer, it was something vague that had made me feel afraid. Now something concrete made me feel afraid – but my fear itself was still vague: what could Marilyn Monroe's death ever have to do with me?

'IT HAS TO DO WITH ALL OF US,' said Owen Meany, when I called him that night. 'SHE WAS JUST LIKE OUR WHOLE COUNTRY – NOT QUITE YOUNG ANYMORE, BUT NOT OLD EITHER; A LITTLE BREATHLESS, VERY BEAUTIFUL, MAYBE A LITTLE STUPID, MAYBE A LOT SMARTER THAN SHE SEEMED, AND SHE WAS LOOKING FOR SOMETHING – I THINK SHE WANTED TO BE GOOD. LOOK AT THE

MEN IN HER LIFE – JOE DIMAGGIO, ARTHUR MILLER, MAYBE THE KENNEDYS. LOOK AT HOW GOOD THEY SEEM! LOOK AT HOW DESIRABLE SHE WAS! THAT'S WHAT SHE WAS: SHE WAS DESIRABLE. SHE WAS FUNNY AND SEXY – AND SHE WAS VULNERABLE, TOO. SHE WAS NEVER QUITE HAPPY, SHE WAS ALWAYS A LITTLE OVERWEIGHT. SHE WAS JUST LIKE OUR WHOLE COUNTRY,' he repeated; he was on a roll. I could hear Hester playing her guitar in the background, as if she were trying to improvise a folk song from everything he said. 'AND THOSE MEN,' he said. 'THOSE FAMOUS, POWERFUL MEN – DID THEY REALLY LOVE HER? DID THEY TAKE CARE OF HER? IF SHE WAS EVER WITH THE KENNEDYS, THEY COULDN'T HAVE LOVED HER – THEY WERE JUST USING HER, THEY WERE JUST BEING CARELESS AND TREATING THEMSELVES TO A THRILL. THAT'S WHAT POWERFUL MEN DO TO THIS COUNTRY – IT'S A BEAUTIFUL, SEXY, BREATHLESS COUNTRY, AND POWERFUL MEN USE IT TO TREAT THEMSELVES TO A THRILL! THEY SAY THEY LOVE IT BUT THEY DON'T MEAN IT. THEY SAY THINGS TO MAKE THEMSELVES APPEAR GOOD – THEY MAKE THEMSELVES APPEAR GOOD – THEY MAKE THEMSELVES APPEAR *MORAL*. THAT'S WHAT I THOUGHT KENNEDY WAS: A MORALIST. BUT HE WAS JUST GIVING US A SNOW JOB, HE WAS JUST BEING A GOOD SEDUCER. I THOUGHT HE WAS A SAVIOR. I THOUGHT HE WANTED TO USE HIS POWER TO DO GOOD. BUT PEOPLE WILL SAY AND DO ANYTHING JUST TO GET POWER; THEN THEY'LL USE THE POWER JUST TO GET A THRILL. MARILYN MONROE WAS ALWAYS LOOKING FOR THE BEST MAN – MAYBE SHE WANTED THE MAN WITH THE MOST ABILITY TO DO GOOD, AND SHE WAS SEDUCED, OVER AND OVER AGAIN – SHE GOT FOOLED, SHE WAS TRICKED, SHE GOT USED, SHE WAS USED UP. JUST LIKE THE COUNTRY. THE COUNTRY WANTS A SAVIOR. THE COUNTRY IS A SUCKER FOR POWERFUL MEN WHO LOOK GOOD. WE THINK THEY'RE MORALISTS AND THEN THEY JUST USE US. THAT'S WHAT'S GOING TO HAPPEN TO YOU AND ME,' said Owen Meany. 'WE'RE GOING TO BE USED.'

Maya Angelou

From 'On the Pulse of Morning' (1993)

On the Pulse of Morning

A Rock, A River, A Tree
Hosts to species long since departed,
Marked the mastodon,
The dinosaur, who left dried tokens
Of their sojourn here
On our planet floor,
Any broad alarm of their hastening doom
Is lost in the gloom of dust and ages.

But today, the Rock cries out to us, clearly, forcefully,
Come, you may stand upon my
Back and face your distant destiny,
But seek no haven in my shadow,
I will give you no hiding place down here...

Across the wall of the world,
A River sings a beautiful song. It says,
Come, rest here by my side.

Each of you, bordered country,
Delicate and strangely made proud,
Yet thrusting perpetually under siege.
Your armed struggles for profit
Have left collars of waste upon
My shore, currents of debris upon my breast.
Yet today I call you to my riverside,
If you will study war no more. ...

There is a true yearning to respond to
The singing River and the wise Rock.
So say the Asian, the Hispanic, the Jew,
The African, the Native American, the Sioux,
The Catholic, the Muslim, the French, the Greek,
The Irish, the Rabbi, the Priest, the Sheik,
The Gay, the Straight, the Preacher,
The privileged, the homeless, the Teacher.
They hear. They all hear
The speaking of the Tree. ...

Come to me,
Here beside the River.
Plant yourself beside the River.

Each of you, descendant of some passed–
On traveler, has been paid for.
You, who gave me my first name, you,
Pawnee, Apache, Seneca, you,
Cherokee Nation, who rested with me, then
Forced on bloody feet,
Left me to the employment of
Other seekers – desperate for gain,
Starving for gold.

You, the Turk, the Arab, the Swede,
The German, the Eskimo, the Scott,
The Italian, the Hungarian, the Pole,
You the Ashanti, the Yoruba, the Kru, bought,
Sold, stolen, arriving on a nightmare,
Praying for a dream.

Here, root yourselves beside me.
I am that Tree planted by the River,
Which will not be moved.
I, the Rock, I, the River, I, the Tree,
I am yours – your passages have been paid.
Lift up your faces, you have a piercing need
For this bright morning dawning for you.
History, despite its wrenching pain,
Cannot be unloved, but if faced
With courage, need not be lived again. ...

Here, on the pulse of this new day,
You may have the grace to look up and out
And into your sister's eyes,
And into your brother's face,
Your country,
And say simply
Very simply
With hope –
Good morning.

George Bilgere

'At the Vietnam Memorial' (1995)

At the Vietnam Memorial

The last time I saw Paul Castle
it was printed in gold on the wall
above the showers in the boy's
locker room, next to the school
record for the mile. I don't recall
his time, but the year was 1968
and I can look across the infield
of memory to see him on the track,
legs flashing, body bending slightly
beyond the pack of runners at his back.

He couldn't spare a word for me,
two years younger, junior varsity,
and hardly worth the waste of breath.
He owned the hallways, a cool blonde
at his side, and aimed his interests
further down the line than we could guess.

Now, reading the name again,
I see us standing in the showers,
naked kids beneath his larger,
comprehensive force – the ones who trail
obscurely, in the wake of the swift,
like my shadow on this gleaming wall.

Don DeLillo

From *Underworld* (1997)

Most of our longings go unfulfilled. This is the word's wistful implication – a desire for something lost or fled or otherwise out of reach.

In Phoenix now, with the years blowing by, I take a drive sometimes out past the regimented typeface on the map and down through the streets named for Indian tribes and past the roofing supply and sandblasting and the condom outlet, painted now in ice-cream flavors, and finally I see the impressive open-steel truss of the waste facility down off Lower Buckeye Road, with grackles sparking across the landfill and the planes in a long line coming out of the hazy mountains to drop into approach patterns.

Marian and I are closer now, more intimate than we've ever been. The serrate edges have dulled away. We go to Tucson to see our daughter and granddaughter. We redecorate our house, building new bookshelves all the time, buying new carpets to set on top of the old ones, and we walk along the drainage canal in the twilight and tell each other stories of the past.

In the bronze tower I stand by the window and look at the hills and ridges and it's a hundred and ten degrees out on the street and I always wear a suit even if I'm only here to check the mail and I listen to the microtonal hum of the systems and feel a quiet kind of power because I've done it and come out okay, done it and won, gone in weak and come out strong, and I do my imitation gangster for the elevator guy.

We separate our household waste accordingly to the guidelines. We rinse out the used cans and empty bottles and put them in their respective bins. We do tin versus aluminum. We use a paper bag for the paper bags, pressing the smaller bags flat and fitting them into the large bag that we've set aside for the purpose. We bundle the newspapers but do not tie them in twine. ...

They are trading garbage in the commodity pits in Chicago. They are making synthetic feces in Dallas. You can sell your testicles to a firm in Russia that will give you four thousands dollars and then remove the items surgically and mash them up and extract the vital substances and market the resulting syrupy stuff as rejuvenating beauty cream, for a profit that is awesome.

We take the TV set out of the cool room at the back of the house, Lainie's old room, our daughter, which is my mother's old room now, the room with the humidifier and the resilvered mirror and the good hard healthy bed, and we build bookshelves there.

At Waste Containment I've become a sort of executive emeritus. I go to the office now and then but mostly travel and speak. I visit colleges and research facilities, where I'm introduced as a waste analyst. I talk to them about the vacated military bases being converted to landfill use, about the bunker system under a mountain in Nevada that will or will not accommodate thousands of steel canisters of radioactive waste for ten thousand years. Then we eat lunch. The waste may or may not explode, seventy thousand tons of spent fuel, and I fly to London and Zurich to attend conferences in the rain and sleet.

I rearrange books on the old shelves and match and mix for the new shelves and then I stand there looking. I stand in the living room and look. Or I walk through the house and look at the things we own and feel the odd mortality that clings to every object. The finer and rarer the object, the more lonely it makes me feel, and I don't know how to account for this. ...

I drive out there sometimes and see grackles sparking across the landfill, down past the Indian tribe streets, and sometimes I take our granddaughter along when she is here on a visit and we see the sage gray truss of the waste facility and the planes in their landing patterns and the showy desert plants spilling over the pastel walls above the parking area.

I fly to Zurich and Lisbon to exchange ideas and make proposals and it is the kind of desperate crisis, the intractability of waste, that doesn't really seem to be taking place except in the conference reports and the newspapers. It is not otherwise touchable somehow, for all the menacing heft and breadth of the material, the actual pulsing thing.

4 How to write about 20th century American literature

Part 4 considers both the task of writing about the literature of this period and the range of critical responses you may find useful in developing your own ideas.

- Where do I start? What sort of text am I dealing with?
- What can I learn from comparing one literary work with another?
- What can I say about the context in which a text was written and in which it may be read?
- How can I evaluate the views of other readers to help me to clarify my own point of view?

Establishing the context

When writing about American literature, it is possible to approach from a number of different directions. You can choose to develop a reading of a work in terms of a fairly narrow context (for instance, another work by the same author) or within a much wider context (for example, other works written at the same time or the author's life). Particular works and authors seem to encourage some approaches rather than others, but it is important to begin with a careful examination of the work itself – although you may later decide that a direct discussion of a work can only come after a specific context has been established.

Basic questions to ask about a literary work might include:

- What is this work about, what is the story (if it has one), what is the subject?
- What is the author saying, what is the work's main idea or theme? What are the author's values? How does the author want the reader to feel about the work?
- How does the author do it – convey facts or feelings or ideas or values? What literary techniques operate to make readers react as they do?

Writing about 20th century American literature involves considering these questions within an historical and cultural context. For example:

- In what ways does this work or author engage with subjects, settings, language and issues that reflect his or her time and place?

- How does the author draw on contemporary or past attitudes and values in terms of his or her material and themes?
- In what ways are the literary techniques in the text new and individual? In what ways are they experimental? In what ways do they reflect the traditions of earlier American writing and thinking?

Such challenging questions help you to look carefully not at single works or authors in isolation but to consider them in comparison with other works and authors. These contextualising questions also encourage you to look at other readers' responses.

Writers' responses to the American experience before the 20th century

As indicated in the passage by Arthur Barlowe (pages 72–73), even before the first white settlers arrived from Europe in large numbers, people struggled to define America. Long before the 20th century, literary men and women – many of whom were also practising poets and novelists – entered the debate and tried to define the role of the American writer. The early Puritans had felt that the Bible was the most important book for all readers. Their own writing thus focused on what they saw as the word of God: their sermons and poetry, journals and diaries, while often chronicling intensely personal experiences and vividly depicting life in the New World, were supposed to direct the reader's attention back to Biblical truths. By the end of the 18th century, however, with the Declaration of Independence in 1776, American writers felt free to take on a new role – but what was that role to be? John Adams, one of the men who signed the Declaration as well as the second President of the United States, wrote to his wife Abigail that he was entering political life so that his sons would have the freedom to become farmers so that their sons, in turn, might have the freedom to become poets. Similarly, Thomas Jefferson, the new nation's third President, did not rank his eight years in this office as his highest achievement. Rather, he requested that the following words appear on his gravestone: 'Author of the Declaration of Independence, of the Statute of Virginia for religious freedom, & Father [that is, founder] of the University of Virginia'. Writers were clearly valued by such leaders, but – after those expressly political documents which defined the nation and its states – what were writers to write? What sort of language should they use? What ought their themes to be? And who would be their readers? Americans throughout the 19th century and into the 20th were, by and large, hard-working people with limited leisure; newspapers flourished in even the most remote settlement, but serious poetry and fiction, despite Adams' and Jefferson's efforts, would need to struggle for a discerning audience. American writers and literary critics have grappled with these issues, and their responses to American literature – their definitions, interpretations and evaluations of it, their prescriptions for what American writers ought to do and their hopes for what the nation's writers might achieve – can help modern readers to clarify and develop their own points of view.

Consider the following statement made by Walt Whitman in 1855:

> The Americans of all nations at any time upon the earth, have probably the fullest poetical nature. The United States themselves are essentially the greatest poem. In the history of the earth hitherto, the largest and most stirring appear tame and orderly to their ampler largeness and stir. Here at last is something in the doings of man that corresponds with the broadcast doings of the day and the night. Here is action untied from strings, necessarily blind to particulars and details, magnificently moving in masses. Here is the hospitality which for ever indicates heroes. Here the performance, disdaining the trivial, unapproach'd in the tremendous audacity of its crowds and groupings, and the push of its perspective, spreads with crampless and flowing breadth, and showers its prolific and splendid extravagance. One sees it must indeed own the riches of the summer and winter, and need never be bankrupt while corn grows from the ground, or the orchards drop apples, or the bays contain fish, or men beget children upon women.
>
> (from the Preface to the first [1855] edition of *Leaves of Grass*)

It is hard to resist the author's confident optimism here, but how accurately does 20th century literature reflect Whitman's vision? How, in fact, do later writers respond to America's 'largeness', to 'action untied from strings', to the 'masses'?

▶ In this context, look at Dos Passos' representation of the country in the passage from *U.S.A.* (pages 33–34). How would you characterise the tone and mood of this extract? How does Whitman's statement help to explain Dos Passos' feelings?

▶ Look also at the extract from Ginsberg's 'Howl' (pages 46–47). What has happened to Whitman's America in Ginsberg's poem? Is Ginsberg criticising Whitman, contradicting him? Does Ginsberg's America in any way bear out Whitman's assertions, specifically his contention that 'Americans of all nations at any time upon the earth, have probably the fullest poetical nature'? Compare Whitman's final sentence with the last line of 'Howl': are these writers saying totally different things? Has America or Americans' vision of it changed completely between 1855 and 1955 – or are there important continuities for the American poet?

▶ What do you suppose Whitman means when he writes that in America one 'need never be bankrupt'? Look at the passages from Olsen's *Yonnondio* (pages 39–40) and from DeLillo's *Underworld* (pages 101–103): how do these very different authors, writing over sixty years apart, confirm or deny Whitman's assertion?

Writers and critics on 20th century American literature

In responding to such questions, in thinking about Whitman's ideas, you can begin to notice and to understand significant continuities – and perhaps also discontinuities – in writers' responses to the American experience.

A critic's views: Alfred Kazin

Like his fellow New Yorker Walt Whitman nearly a century earlier, Alfred Kazin (b.1915), not himself a poet or a novelist but a literary critic throughout his life, also attempted to describe the nature of American literature. In the preface to his important book *On Native Grounds* (1942), Kazin argued that 'the greatest single fact about our modern American writing' is 'our writers' absorption in every last detail of their American world together with their deep and subtle alienation from it'. He found 'a terrible estrangement in this writing, a nameless yearning for a world no one ever really possessed', yet what really interested him was

> ... our alienation on native grounds – the interwoven story of our need to take up our life on our own grounds, and the irony of our possession ... To speak of it only as a struggle toward the modern emancipation – and it was that – does not even hint at the lean and shadowy tragic strain in our modern American writing ... Nor does it tell us why our modern writers have had to discover and rediscover and chart the country in every generation, ... but must still cry America! America! as if we have never known America. As perhaps we have not.

Whitman thought he knew America, but here Kazin suggests that every generation of American writers continues the struggle to 'know' it, to describe it and to come to terms with it over and over again. On the basis of Kazin's statements, how does 20th century American literature illustrate this struggle? You might consider, for instance, how such different works as Henry James' *The Portrait of a Lady* (1881), Theodore Dreiser's *Sister Carrie* (1900), Edith Wharton's *The Age of Innocence* (1920) or Fitzgerald's *The Great Gatsby* (1925) explore the problem of the alienated American at the same time that they offer us a detailed portrait of 'their American world'. You might look at what Kazin is saying in relation to the poetry of T.S. Eliot or Robert Lowell or in relation to the work of such playwrights as Arthur Miller or

David Mamet (b. 1947). You may decide that a critic is brilliantly insightful, only partially correct – or even wrong. Thinking seriously about such ideas and examining how they might illuminate a particular text can enrich understanding both of the text itself and of the possible contexts within which it can be understood.

Kazin's literary criticism offers a social or cultural context for reading 20th century American literature, but he was also aware that while 'We are all bound up with society, ... we can never forget that literature is not produced by "society", but by a succession of individuals and out of individual sensibility and knowledge and craft.' (from the preface to *On Native Grounds*). Prose as well as poetry needs to be considered from the perspective of 'craft', from the perspective of word choice and sentence structure and overall form. Poetry in particular demands this attention, because of its often shorter length and its concentration of thought and feeling.

Views of a particular poem: H.D.'s 'Oread'

Although critics may disagree, their views of a particular poem can often help you to notice things you might not otherwise see. Consider, for example, these different approaches to H.D.'s 'Oread' (page 80):

1 Ezra Pound set 'Oread' within the context of the literary movement that in 1912 he called **Imagism**. For him, H.D.'s poem above all illustrates the movement's principles, among them: direct treatment of the 'thing'; objectivity; the expression of an 'intellectual and emotional complex'; even 'one idea set on top of another'. (from Ezra Pound *Gaudier-Brzeska: A Memoir*, 1916)

2 Jeanne Kammer also sees the poem as an illustration of Ezra Pound's modernist idea of the 'image', but she points out as well that 'Oread' uses a special sort of metaphor which does not, like most metaphors, move from concrete to abstract, but rather depends on the 'juxtaposition and suspension of concrete elements' in a single 'configuration'. (from Jeanne Kammer 'The Art of Silence and the Forms of Women's Poetry', in *Shakespeare's Sisters: Feminist Essays on Women Poets*, 1979)

3 Gary Burnett suggests that 'Oread' is an important 'imagist' poem, but also 'an important component of a broadly conceived sequence'. In fact, Burnett insists, all of H.D.'s 'poems – from the shortest to the longest – exist in context rather than in isolation, both as part of the particular volumes in which they [first] appear and in the larger pattern of H.D.'s ongoing poetic explorations'. (from Gary Burnett *H.D. between Image and Epic: The Mysteries of Her Poetics*, 1990)

4 Susan Stanford Friedman has written at length about 'Oread':

> Since most imagist poems present images from nature, it is easy to assume that imagist poetry is about nature. But 'Oread' and most of H.D.'s imagist poems ... are about consciousness, not the world of

> objects external to consciousness. The center of 'Oread', as the title indicates, is not the sea; it is instead the perceptions and emotions of an oread, a nymph of the mountains, as she regards the sea in a whirling passion of intensity ... the poem presents images of the sea in order to embody an 'intellectual and emotional complex', which is the real subject of the poem.
>
> The images that simultaneously obscure and reveal the emotions of the oread are not surrealist images emerging from the unconscious. 'Oread' is a controlled poem ... But the waves made of pine trees and the trees made of water have a quality analogous to the dream ... The poem significantly does not rely upon similes, which by definition remind the reader that the images only make comparisons, not equivalences. The speaker does not say that a rough sea looks like pointed trees; she *sees* tree-waves ...
>
> ... The oread *is* the land and consequently identifies with the shore and addresses the waves as 'you'. As the spirit of the land, she understandably perceives her fluid opposite in her own terms: waves are pointed pines that whirl up, crash, and make pools of fir. This nonrational mode of thought gives motion, fury, and a watery stillness to the land; conversely, it gives stature and stability to the sea. But these images condense opposites into a contradictory whole; they simultaneously affirm and deny the division of land and sea.

Friedman concludes that 'the fusion of land and sea in "Oread" does not in itself explain the emotional intensity of the poem', and goes on to suggest a sexual dimension:

> The oread's commands throughout the poem emphasise that the sea acts while the land is acted upon. H.D.'s images may be identifying a traditional masculinity with the waves (movement; sexual assault) and a traditional femininity with the land (passivity; sexual receptivity).

Friedman finally decides that 'The ultimate subject of the poem is the consciousness of the poet herself'. (from Susan Stanford Friedman *Psyche Reborn: The Emergence of H.D.*, 1981)

What are these critics asking the reader to do? Pound suggests that it is necessary to know more about his literary movement in order to understand his poems. You might do this by looking, for instance, at a biography of Pound. Burnett encourages readers to seek out H.D.'s *Sea Garden* (1916), the collection of verse in which 'Oread' first appeared, in order to understand this poem as part of a 'larger pattern'. Helpfully, H.D.'s *Collected Poems* contains this volume in its entirety.

Kammer directs attention to the figurative language in 'Oread' and points out how she feels the central comparison works. Are you persuaded by her analysis of the 'juxtaposition and suspension of concrete elements' in a single 'configuration'?

Friedman's extensive discussion should make you measure each of her assertions against your own reading of the poem's figurative language, images and themes: do you agree or disagree? Do you find Friedman partly right? In what ways would you add to or qualify her interpretations?

Finally, what do you make of the contradictions among these critics? Does Pound help you to understand H.D. or does he really tell you more about himself as a poet? What do you make of his contention that 'Oread' is 'objective' while Friedman emphasises the nymph's point of view and insists that the poem is ultimately about the poet's own consciousness?

Secondary sources

Making the best use of secondary sources – such as these on H.D. – may be a challenging task, for it involves careful, discriminating reading and occasionally some extra research, but it can be extremely rewarding. Reading what critics have to say about literature is finally not about what the critics' have to say, but about what you yourself think and feel. Any meaningful encounter with critical material will send you back to the author and the literary text itself.

As Kazin points out, all literary work depends not only on 'knowledge and craft' but on 'individual sensibility'. Secondary material which helps the reader to understand a particular text and the sensibility that created it can be of various sorts. It can be literary criticism of the kind presented above on H.D., or it may be more obviously biographical. For instance, it is difficult to read Sylvia Plath's writing today without an awareness of her suicide, and it may be useful to know more about the life which often figures so explicitly as the subject of her work. It might help to read what biographers have said about her childhood in Massachusetts; her mental breakdown during her university years; her experience at Newnham College, Cambridge; her marriage to the British poet Ted Hughes; her experiences as a young mother of two small children; her decision to remain in England rather than to return to the United States; her final, creative months in Devon and London just before her death in 1963. You may want to read not only what biographers have written, but what Plath's husband has had to say about their relationship. Hughes has written prefaces to Plath's work and made a number of statements quoted in biographies, but he has also published *Birthday Letters* (1998), a volume of poems about Plath. You may want to read what Plath herself has said about her life and work. *Letters Home* (1975), her letters to her mother covering more than a decade, reveal a carefully shaped version of herself for a particular audience. There are two different editions of *The Journals*: one edited by Hughes (1983) and another, three times as long, edited by Karen V. Kukil (2000). However, not all biographers will agree, and even – or perhaps especially – people who knew the author well will have different versions of her and different reasons for expressing them. Authors themselves also have agendas: what Plath writes to her mother is often very different from what she confides to her diary, while the published journals are only a partial selection and reflect the editor's judgement. Anyone interested in biography and autobiography as a way into any text, as an approach to the writer's 'individual sensibility', will have to read just as critically as when using other secondary sources. Nevertheless, the rewards can be revealing, helping readers to see literary work within a particularly rich and personal context.

The author's own views

Consider as an example of an author's own views these statements by Fitzgerald about *The Great Gatsby*. The first is taken from a letter to his editor, Max Perkins, on 16 April 1924:

> While I have every hope and plan of finishing my novel in June, you know how those things often come out, and even if it takes me ten times that long I cannot let it go unless it has the very best I'm capable of in it, or even, as I feel sometimes, something better than I'm capable of. Much of what I wrote last summer was good but it was so interrupted that it was ragged and, in approaching it from a new angle, I've had to discard a lot of it – in one case 18,000 words [this became the short story 'Absolution'] ... I feel I have enormous power in me now, more than I've ever had in a way, but it works so fitfully and with so many bogeys because I've *talked so much* and not lived enough within myself to develop the necessary self-reliance. Also I don't know anyone who has used up so much personal experience as I have at 27 ... So in my new novel I'm thrown directly on purely creative work – not trashy imaginings as in my stories but the sustained imagination of a sincere yet radiant world. ... This book will be a consciously artistic achievement and must depend on that ...

After *Gatsby*'s publication in the spring of 1925, Fitzgerald thanked his university friend, the critic Edmund Wilson, for his comments:

> I was awfully happy that you liked it and that you approved of the design. The worst fault in it, I think is a BIG FAULT: I gave no account (and had no feeling about or knowledge of) the emotional relations between Gatsby and Daisy from the time of their reunion to the catastrophe. However, the lack is so astutely concealed by the retrospect of Gatsby's past and by blankets of excellent prose that no one has noticed it ...

To his friend John Peale Bishop, a fellow novelist, Fitzgerald wrote on 9 August 1925:

> Thank you for your most pleasant, full, discerning and helpful letter about *The Great Gatsby* ... you are right about Gatsby being blurred and patchy. I never at any one time saw him clear myself – for he started as one man I knew and then changed into myself – the amalgam was never complete in my mind. (from *The Letters of F. Scott Fitzgerald*, ed. Andrew Turnbull, 1963)

What do these extracts say about Fitzgerald's attitude towards his masterpiece? What does he say that surprises you? What do his comments reveal about the creative process? The discarded material, which became the short story 'Absolution', is a compelling account of a young boy in moral and emotional conflict and his relationship with the Catholic priest to whom he goes for confession. Reading this story may help you to understand Gatsby's background – or you may decide that Fitzgerald was right to delete it. Further knowledge of Fitzgerald's life may help you to evaluate his comment to Bishop – that Gatsby is both 'one man' he knew and himself – and to decide to what extent the author's perception here adds to your appreciation of this character. Do you agree with Fitzgerald about what he called the novel's 'BIG FAULT'? Fitzgerald also draws attention in these letters to *The Great Gatsby* as a 'consciously artistic achievement', a work that depends on 'design': are you aware of this while reading the novel? What do you gain by thinking about the text in these terms? Fitzgerald's letters and the questions they encourage suggest valuable and interesting perspectives beyond those you may have considered when reading *The Great Gatsby* for the first time.

Reading and rereading texts in different eras

This act of reading and rereading, of thinking about a text, doing some research, and then rethinking approaches and conclusions, brings up another important point about how to approach literature. Clearly a reader's understanding of a text is a process and changes over time. This is also true of critics' responses. Thus a writer's reputation may fluctuate, developing in often surprising ways from decade to decade, and it is possible to speak of a writer's 'reception'. The history of how an author's work has been read by others over a particular period reveals as much about how different readers are shaped by their own times as it does about the literary work itself. An awareness of an author's reception should make the reader aware of both the cultural and individual attitudes that influence his or her own reading. Such an awareness should demonstrate as well the importance of not taking another person's word for it, the importance of reading and thinking carefully, responsibly and independently. For instance, Susan Beegal has pointed out that Hemingway's reputation has for years depended in large measure on an 'almost exclusively male critical hierarchy' who 'sometimes carried on like guys in a locker room'. Beegal explains:

> With their pronouncements unleavened by feminist thought and unchallenged by feminist colleagues, some early male critics of Hemingway man-handled his striking women characters and ignored those stories where he wrote with sensitivity from a woman's point of view. ...
>
> The dearth of minorities and women in the academy during the 1960s is probably the most significant negative influence on Hemingway's critical reputation today. When potential readers reject Hemingway as indifferent to minorities and hostile to women, they are often responding not to Hemingway's fiction, but to the indifference and hostility of some of his early critics, and a negative image of the author those influential first admirers unintentionally projected. (from Susan F. Beegel 'Conclusion: The Critical Reputation of Ernest Hemingway', in *The Cambridge Companion to Ernest Hemingway*, 1996)

Hemingway is a striking case, but many other writers have similarly experienced significant 'rereadings' because of a changed climate of opinion. Another example is Zora Neale Hurston, whose work was nearly forgotten until she was 'rediscovered' in the 1970s. The careers of black authors throughout the 20th century may make the modern reader wonder about Whitman's contention that 'Here is the hospitality which for ever indicates heroes.' In fact, many American writers of colour, women writers, Jewish writers, homosexual or lesbian writers, immigrant writers and writers from backgrounds of poverty or other sorts of 'difference' have suffered the fate of being misread or even of not being read at all. If they are lucky, like Hurston and Hemingway, they get 'reread'. Consider, for example, these comments from the foreword to Adrienne Rich's first volume of poetry, *A Change of World* (1951), by the British poet W.H. Auden:

> Miss Rich, who is, I understand, twenty-one years old, displays a modesty not so common at that age, which disclaims any extraordinary vision, and a love for her medium, a determination to ensure that whatever she writes shall, at least, not be shoddily made. In a young poet ... the most promising sign is craftsmanship for it is evidence of a capacity for detachment from the self and its emotions without which no art is possible. ...
>
> I suggested at the beginning of this introduction that poems are

> analogous to persons; the poems the reader will encounter in this book are neatly and modestly dressed, speak quietly but do not mumble, respect their elders but are not cowed by them, and do not tell fibs ...

This condescending evaluation of Rich's work reveals more about what was expected of a young woman in 1950s America than about the poems themselves. Auden describes the poet and her poems as if they were potentially unruly and offensive children who had learned just enough about appropriate behaviour to be allowed into a Victorian drawing room. Thus he praises Rich for such traditionally feminine virtues as modesty and self-denial. He further trivialises her work by speaking of it as a barely civilised guest at a tea party: neatly and modestly dressed, speaking quietly but not mumbling, respecting its elders and not telling 'fibs'. Even the childish word 'fibs' serves to belittle Rich's achievement.

The American poet Randall Jarrell, reviewing Rich's second book, *The Diamond Cutters and Other Poems* (1956), was no more enlightened:

> Adrienne Cecil Rich is an enchanting poet; everybody seems to admit it; and this seems only right. Everybody thinks young things young, Sleeping Beauty beautiful – and the poet whom we see behind the clarity and gravity of Miss Rich's poems cannot help seeming to us a sort of princess in a fairy tale. Her scansion, even, is easy and limpid, close to water, close to air; she lives nearer to perfection... than ordinary poets do, and her imperfections themselves are touching as the awkwardness of anything young and natural is touching. The reader feels she has only begun to change; thinks, 'This young thing, who knows what it may be, old?'

Here Rich and her work have become flower fairies, 'things' as insubstantial as water and air, trivialised as nearly perfect, cute in their tiny failures. Jarrell concludes: 'It seems to me that she herself is, often, a good poet who is all too good – one who can afford to be wild tomorrow; meanwhile, today, she is also an endearing and delightful poet, one who deserves Shakespeare's favorite adjective, *sweet*.' The critic perceives that there may well be more to Rich than the juvenile charmer he insists upon; he correctly suspects that Rich in her early work is indeed restraining herself, as she felt she had to do, in form, subject and theme. But Jarrell's praise of Rich as 'endearing', 'delightful' and above all '*sweet*' must seem today outrageously sexist and patronising.

▶ What words would you use to characterise Rich's 'An Unsaid Word' (page 56) and 'Aunt Jennifer's Tigers' (page 91), both published in 1951?

▶ How well do Auden's and Jarrell's evaluations apply to Rich's later verse, such as

'Twenty-One Love Poems' (one of which appears on page 91) or 'The Burning of Paper Instead of Children' (pages 56–57)? What features of these poems do Auden and Jarrell overlook or distort or misunderstand? Do you feel they actually misrepresent Rich?

▶ What ideas and standards do Auden and Jarrell bring to their mid-century criticism which we – and Rich – might question at the beginning of the 21st century? What does our current awareness of such issues as gender, feminism, sexual orientation, and oppression add to our understanding of her work?

When asked in an interview in 1991, 'Would you prefer to start with literature or politics?' Rich responded, 'We'll get to both, I'm sure; so start wherever you like.' Why do you suppose, given what you now know about 20th century American literature and its many possible contexts, that Rich answered in this way?

Rich herself has written not only poetry but numerous thoughtful essays about literature as well as about larger cultural issues affecting her as an American female poet in the second half of the 20th century. She has also spoken out about her own life. Reread Rich's statement quoted in the introduction to this volume (page 8). How did you feel as you first read Rich's statement? Do you read it differently now?

When Whitman wrote so confidently that the United States of all nations had 'the fullest poetical nature', he implied that America would encourage literature, both the writing of it and the reading of it. Do you think this has been so in the 20th century? Considering all you have learned about American literature and about reading in context, look finally at what Rich says about language:

> I've written a great deal about the whole issue of dead language, the oppressor's language, a language that is no longer useful, and the need to try to find a new language, a common language. ... It's the question of associations with words and of the history of words, and how they come down to us and how we go on with them. But I'm beginning to think and talk a lot more again about that which goes along with language and poetry – which is music, the vibration of a voice. I see that intonation, that vocal quality, as something that is very personal, out of the self, and then combines with the many traditions, the many histories that we've been exposed to, that we come out of. (quoted in Adrienne Rich 'An Interview with David Montenegro', in *Adrienne Rich's Poetry and Prose*, 1993)

Because language itself carries with it a whole history of contexts, Rich indicates that what writers intend and what readers understand may be entirely different things. She also suggests that even just by reading a work of literature out loud, trying to capture in speech what a reader thinks the author may have meant, he or she is bringing to the text something very personal which nevertheless brings with it 'the many traditions, the many histories that we've been exposed to, that we come out of'.

▶ Choose any poem or passage from this volume and read it aloud. Listen to a friend reading it aloud. What do you hear in your own or your friend's voice which adds to – or subtracts from – what you think the text does and says? Is the voice male or female? Old or young? Is the accent American?

To read 20th century American literature is inevitably to read it in context. Part of your responsibility in writing about literature, then, is to reflect not only on what you feel the author is saying, but on the rich range of contexts that you bring out of your own life to any text you read.

Assignments

1 Look at the passages by Barlowe (pages 72–73), Whitman (pages 73–75), Jewett (pages 76–77), Lewis (pages 83–85) and DeLillo (pages 101–103). Each of these authors explores a particular American landscape. In Jewett's case, the 'landscape' is the very small garden at the back of a New England village house; for Barlowe and Whitman, the landscape is large and expansive.

How is America portrayed by each of these authors? Consider the passages' subject, language, and tone. What attitudes does each writer or speaker have towards the land itself? What similarities and differences do you notice? On the basis of these selections, what differences in the depiction of American landscape occur over time? Consider carefully what you know about the context in which these pieces were written. What conclusions can you draw?

2 Walt Whitman has had a significant influence on writers throughout the 20th century. Consider Pound's 'A Pact' (page 80), Sandburg's 'Happiness' (page 81), Hughes' 'I, Too' (pages 37–38) and Ginsberg's 'A Supermarket in California' (pages 87–88). In what ways do these authors respond to Whitman in their work? Look at both what is actually stated about Whitman in some of these poems and at the ways in which these authors draw on Whitman in their use of language, rhythm, syntax,

form and subject matter. Does Whitman seem to have continued relevance for American authors? Support your response with specific evidence.

3 A number of authors in this book are represented by several passages or poems. Consider, for example, Pound, Frost, Sandburg, Plath, Rich or Li-Young Lee. What common elements characterise an individual author's work? Consider subjects, use of language and themes. Can you see any changes over time in the work of Frost or Rich?

You may wish to develop your own responses by reading additional writing by these authors or other authors mentioned in this volume. What sort of writer, for example, is Pound or Lee? What impression of them do you get when you read ten or twelve of their poems? Support your generalisations with specific evidence from their work.

4 Many American writers are interested in the vernacular, in language as it is actually spoken, as an important element in national identity. Look at several authors who use a first-person speaker who addresses the reader directly. Examine the different voices, for instance, in Clifton's 'Richard Penniman' (page 90), and in Alice Walker's novel *The Color Purple*. Consider how these authors set up a dramatic situation. How do these writers reveal character as well as the speaker's background – including in some instances region, class, race, and gender – not only through specific details but through word choice and sentence structure?

5 Workers figure as subjects in a number of 20th century American texts. Look at male and female workers in works by one or more writers, for example, Upton Sinclair, Robert Frost, Carl Sandburg, Sinclair Lewis, John Dos Passos, Arthur Miller, Tillie Olsen, or Annie Proulx. What does their treatment of working people reveal about the problems and tensions in American life?

6 Go to your local travel agent and pick up some brochures about the United States. What do the pictures and the written advertising stress about America? How accurate an impression is this, do you feel, on the basis of the authors you have read? What seems 'spot on'? What are these brochures omitting? What differences in tone do you notice between these brochures and the work of the writers you have studied?

5 Resources

Chronology of writers and texts

1899	Kate Chopin *The Awakening*
1901	Booker T. Washington *Up from Slavery*
1903	W.E.B. Du Bois *The Souls of Black Folk*
1912	H.D.'s and Pound's Imagist verse published in *Poetry Magazine* in Chicago
1913	Robert Frost *A Boy's Will*
1914	First Imagist anthology *Des Imagistes*
1916	H.D. *Sea Garden*
1919	Sherwood Anderson *Winesburg, Ohio*
1920	Ezra Pound 'Hugh Selwyn Mauberly'
1922	T.S. Eliot *The Waste Land*; James Joyce *Ulysses*
1925	F. Scott Fitzgerald *The Great Gatsby*; Ernest Hemingway *In Our Time* published in Paris; John Dos Passos *Manhattan Transfer*
1926	Ernest Hemingway *The Sun Also Rises*; Carl Sandburg begins his multi-volume biography of Abraham Lincoln
1929	William Faulkner *The Sound and the Fury*; Ernest Hemingway *A Farewell to Arms*; Virginia Woolf *A Room of One's Own*
1935	T.S. Eliot *Murder in the Cathedral*; Clifford Odets *Waiting for Lefty*
1937	Zora Neale Hurston *Their Eyes Were Watching God*
1940	Richard Wright *Native Son*
1942	Alfred Kazin *On Native Grounds*
1945	Tennessee Williams *The Glass Menagerie*
1946	Carson McCullers *The Member of the Wedding*
1947	Arthur Miller *All My Sons*
1948	Norman Mailer *The Naked and the Dead*; Ezra Pound *The Pisan Cantos*
1949	Arthur Miller *Death of a Salesman*
1951	Adrienne Rich *A Change of World*; David Riesman *The Lonely Crowd*; J.D. Salinger *The Catcher in the Rye*
1952	Ralph Ellison *Invisible Man*
1953	Arthur Miller *The Crucible*
1955	James Baldwin *Notes of a Native Son*; Emily Dickinson *Complete Poems*, ed. Thomas H. Johnson
1956	Allen Ginsberg 'Howl'
1957	Bernard Malamud *The Assistant*

1959 Philip Roth *Goodbye, Columbus*
1960 Harper Lee *To Kill a Mockingbird*; H.D. *Bid Me to Live*
1961 Joseph Heller *Catch-22*
1963 James Baldwin *The Fire Next Time*
1964 Ernest Hemingway *A Moveable Feast*; Malcolm X *The Autobiography*
1965 Sylvia Plath *Ariel*
1968 Norman Mailer *Armies of the Night*
1974 Tillie Olsen *Yonnondio*
1976 Marilyn French *The Women's Room*
1982 Alice Walker *The Color Purple*
1987 Toni Morrison *Beloved*
1989 Susan Sontag *AIDS and its Metaphors*
1997 Philip Roth *American Pastoral*
1998 Don DeLillo *Underworld*
1999 Adrienne Rich *Midnight Salvage*

Other literary dates

1908 Ezra Pound leaves America to live in Europe
1910 Mark Twain dies
1911 H.D. leaves America to live in Europe
1914 T.S. Eliot leaves America to live abroad
1916 Henry James dies
1921–1928 Ernest Hemingway lives in Paris
1924–1931 F. Scott Fitzgerald lives in France
1930 Sinclair Lewis awarded the Nobel Prize for Literature
1932 Tillie Olsen begins *Yonnondio*
1940 F. Scott Fitzgerald dies in Hollywood
1945–1958 Ezra Pound in St. Elizabeth's Hospital for the criminally insane in Washington, D.C.
1947 Richard Wright leaves America to live in Paris
1948 James Baldwin leaves America to live in Paris
1950 William Faulkner awarded the Nobel Prize for Literature
1954 Ernest Hemingway awarded the Nobel Prize for Literature
1957 Arthur Miller convicted of contempt of Congress for refusing to name suspected communists
1961 Ernest Hemingway dies
1963 Sylvia Plath dies
1966 Le Roi Jones changes his name to Imamu Amiri Baraka
1976 Saul Bellow awarded the Nobel Prize for Literature
1993 Toni Morrison awarded the Nobel Prize for Literature
1999 The Metropolitan Opera concludes the century with a premiere of an operatic version of *The Great Gatsby*

Further reading

Books by individual authors are listed in the Chronology (see page 118).

Secondary texts

William L. Andrews, et al, eds. *The Oxford Companion to African American Literature* (Oxford University Press, 1997)
A 'dictionary' of black writing, art, history and culture in America. Entries on individual authors; also the civil rights movement and the Harlem renaissance.

Malcolm Bradbury and Richard Ruland *From Puritanism to Post Modernism: A History of American Literature* (Penguin, 1991)

Clive Bloom and Brian Docherty, eds. *American Poetry: The Modernist Ideal* (Macmillan, 1995)
A collection of essays on, among others, H.D., Pound, Stevens, cummings, Williams, and Ginsberg.

Cathy Davidson and Linda Wagner-Martin, eds. *The Oxford Companion to Women's Writing in the United States* (Oxford University Press, 1995)
A 'dictionary' of women's writing in America from the 17th–20th centuries. Entries on individual authors, and on social and cultural topics affecting female writers.

Morris Dickstein *Gates of Eden: American Culture in the Sixties* (New York: Basic Books, 1977)
An inclusive, impressionistic view of the period.

Leslie Fiedler *Love and Death in the American Novel* (Paladin, 1970)
An important study of characters and themes in 19th and 20th century American literature.

James D. Hart, ed. *The Oxford Companion to American Literature* (Oxford University Press, 1995)
An extremely useful 'dictionary' of American literature from the 17th–20th centuries. Biographical entries on individual writers, and on specific works and literary movements.

Gordon Hutner *American Literature, American Culture* (Oxford University Press, 1999)

An anthology of classic essays on the range of American literature from its beginnings to the end of the 20th century.

Hugh Kenner *A Homemade World: The American Modernist Writers* (Marion Boyers, 1977)
A study of selected modernist poets and novelists, 1910–1960.

Alfred Kazin *On Native Grounds* (New York: Harcourt Brace Jovanovich, 1970)
A collection of reflective essays which set American literature within a cultural context.

Michael Levinson, ed. *The Cambridge Companion to Modernism* (Cambridge University Press, 1999)
A collection of essays on British and American writers in the first half of the 20th century. Also includes a useful chronological table.

Tillie Olsen *Silences* (Virago, 1980)
A collection of essays on American women authors and on the challenges facing them as both women and writers.

Douglas Tallack *Twentieth Century America: The Intellectual and Cultural Context* (Longman, 1991)

Alice Walker *In Search of Our Mother's Gardens* (The Women's Press, 1984)
Personal essays both on her own development as a writer and on black literature generally.

Computer resources

Websites and CD-ROMS offer interesting new ways to access information about literature. A useful CD-ROM is *Contemporary Authors,* which offers brief biographical entries with commentary on thousands of 20th century writers.

The Internet has become increasingly useful for students of literature, and websites of all sorts and of every quality abound. A sample of some particularly fine ones for readers interested in particular topics or authors is indicated below. These sites can be especially helpful in providing biographical and bibliographical information. Sometimes websites include E-texts (on-line reproductions of poems, short stories and even complete novels) or hypertexts (reproduced texts with scholarly emendations and commentary).

Suggested websites

American Literature: 20th Century Texts and Resources
http://xroads.virginia.edu/~yp/litlink.html
Links to sites for most of the authors mentioned in this book.

Annotated Index of Websites on Modernism
http://www.modcult.brown.edu/people/Scholes/modlist/Title.html
Links to a large number of other sites, for which it offers descriptive and critical notes.

F. Scott Fitzgerald Centenary Home Page
http://www.sc.edu/fitzgerald
Includes biographical information, literary criticism, background to the author's life and times, E-texts of his work and images.

The Papa Page
http://www.ee.mcgill.ca/~nverer/hem/pindex.html
This site on Ernest Hemingway is somewhat quirky, but includes a great deal of interesting information in a compelling format.

The Robert Frost Web Page
http://www.pro-net.co.uk/home/catalyst/RF/rfcover.html
Includes biographical and bibliographical information as well as images and interviews.

Sylvia Plath Home Page
http://ilabws.informatik.uni-leipzig.de/~beckmann/plath.html
A well-organised site with biographical information and images.

William Faulkner on the Web
http://www.mcsr.olemiss.edu/~egjbp/faulkner/faulkner.html
Includes numerous links to other relevant sites as well as biography, criticism, images, bibliographical information and material on Faulkner's work in Hollywood.

Zora Neale Hurston
http://pages.prodigy.com/zora
Includes biographical and bibliographical information as well as images and links to related sites offering additional literary and cultural background.

Glossary of critical terms

Allusion an indirect reference, generally to a person, place or literary work, which enriches the reading context by calling up a set of associations.

Diction word choice. Diction usually involves connotative language which conveys a level of formality (or informality) and often suggests the age, class, race, gender, regional background and education of the speaker (or narrator) and, sometimes, the listener (or reader).

Form the structure and/or conventions employed in a literary work, especially poetry. Poets may write in traditional or fixed form (e.g. the sonnet) or set aside conventions (e.g. rhyme and meter) to develop new forms. In prose, writers may employ formal conventions (e.g. complete sentences or chronological narratives) or they may experiment.

Free verse poetry which rejects traditional rhyme and meter, generally in favour of natural speech rhythms.

Genre (adjective: generic) a type or category of literary expression, such as poetry, fiction, biography or drama.

Gloss a brief explanatory note to clarify a difficult or technical expression.

Imagism the literary movement publicised by Ezra Pound in 1912; its initial proponents included H.D. and the English poet Richard Aldington. Its rules remained vague, but in general it involved writing free verse which rebelled in subject and word choice against what these poets saw as the sentimentality and vagueness of the 19th century.

Irony the contrast between what one might expect and what actually occurs. In literature, irony often depends not only on events but on the use of words to convey the opposite of their literal meaning.

Juxtaposition the placing of two things (or words or concepts) side by side, usually to show contrast.

Meter the regular pattern of stressed and unstressed syllables, usually in a poem.

Modernism the movement in the visual arts, literature and music which broke established rules of form and/or subject matter at the beginning of the 20th century.

Imagism, for example, was one of the first modernist movements in English and American literature.

Mood the emotional atmosphere created in a literary work. The creation of mood frequently depends on the author's use of language.

Naturalism the American literary movement at the end of the 19th and the beginning of the 20th century whose writers suggested that events were determined by forces beyond the individual's control.

Protagonist the central character, who may or may not be a male or female hero.

Realism the American literary movement in the last decades of the 19th and the first years of the 20th century which emphasised ordinary life as it actually was. Realism encouraged authors to use vernacular speech and to focus on everyday events and characters.

Regionalism the American literary movement which encouraged authors to write about particular areas of the United States in order to depict local geography, speech, attitudes and ways of life.

Stream of consciousness an experimental way of writing about what goes on inside characters' heads. It generally involves the breakdown of formal conventions and may consist of a series of long sentences or sentence fragments whose logic is emotional rather than rational.

Syntax the way in which words are put together to form phrases and sentences.

Tone an author's manner of expression. It generally conveys emotional attitudes and in a literary work depends on word choice. We might say that a writer's tone is serious, sarcastic or humorous.

Tradition(s) the conventions, developed over a long period, which characterise a way of thinking about particular topics or a way of writing in a given form. For example, we might speak of the poetic tradition, suggesting (among other things) verse with regular rhyme and meter.

Vernacular ordinary speech, especially the actual language or way of speaking in a particular geographical area.

Vignette a brief literary sketch, often a miniature story whose impact depends on detail rather than on plot or character development.

Index

Acknowledgements

The author and publishers wish to thank the following for permission to use copyright material:

BOA Editions Ltd for extracts from Li-Young Lee, 'Eating Alone' and Li-Young Lee, 'Eating Together' from *The Rose* (1986). Copyright © 1986 by Li-Young Lee; and Lucille Clifton, 'richard penniman' from *Good Women: Poems and a Memoir 1969–1980* (1972). Copyright © 1987 by Lucille Clifton; Carcanet Press and New Directions Publishing Corporation for William Carlos Williams, 'The Red Wheelbarrow' from *Collected Poems: 1909–1939, Vol. 1.* Copyright © 1938 by New Directions Publishing Corporation; and H D Doolittle, 'Oread' from *Collected Poems 1912–1944*. Copyright © 1982 by The Estate of Hilda Doolittle; Gerald Duckworth & Co Ltd and Viking Penguin, a division of Penguin Putnam Inc, for Dorothy Parker, 'General Review of the Sex Situation' from *The Portable Dorothy Parker* by Dorothy Parker. Copyright © 1926, renewed © 1954 by Dorothy Parker; Faber & Faber Ltd for Ezra Pound, 'In A Station of the Metro' and 'A Pact' from *Collected Shorter Poems* by Ezra Pound; with Alfred A Knopf, a division of Random House, Inc, for Wallace Stevens, 'The Death of a Soldier' and an extract from 'Thirteen Ways of Looking at a Blackbird' from *Collected Poems* by Wallace Stevens. Copyright © 1923, renewed © 1951 by Wallace Stevens; and with HarperCollins Publishers, Inc for Sylvia Plath, 'The Applicant'. Copyright © 1963 by Ted Hughes, renewed, and an extract from 'Lesbos'. Copyright © 1963 by Ted Hughes, from *Collected Poems* by Sylvia Plath; Harcourt, Inc for Carl Sandburg, 'Fog', 'Salvage' and 'Happiness' from *Chicago Poems* by Carl Sandburg. Copyright © 1916 by Holt, Rinehart and Winston, renewed © 1944 by Carl Sandburg; from *Songlines in Michaeltree*. Copyright 2000 by Michael S. Harper. Used with permission of the Poet and the University of Illinois Press. Bloomsbury and HarperCollins Publishers, Inc for an extract from John Irving, *A Prayer for Owen Meany*, Bloomsbury (1989). Copyright © 1989 by John Irving; Hemingway Foreign Rights Trust and Scribner, a division of Simon & Schuster, for an extract from Ernest Hemingway, *A Moveable Feast*. Copyright © 1964 by Mary Hemingway, renewed © 1992 by John H Hemingway, Patrick Hemingway and Gregory Hemingway; David Higham Associates on behalf of the Estates of the authors with Alfred A Knopf, Inc, a division of Random House, Inc, for Langston Hughes, 'I, Too' from *Collected Poems* by Langston Hughes. Copyright © 1994 by the Estate of Langston Hughes; with Scribner, a division of Simon & Schuster, for an extract from Fitzgerald letter of April 16, 1924 to Maxwell Perkins from *The Letters of F Scott Fitzgerald*. Copyright © 1963 by Frances Scott Fitzgerald Lanahan, renewed © 1991 by Joanne J Turnbull, Joanne T Turnbull, Frances L Turnbull and Eleanor Lanahan, Matthew J Bruccoli, Samuel J Lanahan, Sr, Trustees u/a dated 7.3.75, created by Frances Scott Fitzgerald Smith; and with New Directions Publishing Corporation for extracts from letters in F Scott Fitzgerald, *The Crack-Up*. Copyright © 1945 by New Directions Publishing Corporation; Macmillan for extracts from Don DeLillo, *Underworld* (1997) pp. 803–5; W W Norton & Company, Inc and the author for Adrienne Rich, 'Poem XII' from 'Twenty-One Love Poems' and 'For Ethel Rosenberg' from *The Fact of a Doorframe: Poems Selected and New*, 1950–1984 by Adrienne Rich. Copyright © 1984 by Adrienne Rich. Copyright © 1975, 1978 by W W Norton & Company, Inc Copyright © 1981 by Adrienne Rich; 'Aunt Jennifer's Tigers'. Copyright © 1993, 1951 by Adrienne Rich; 'An Unsaid Word'. Copyright © 1993, 1951 by Adrienne Rich; lines from 'Planetarium'. Copyright © 1993 by Adrienne Rich. Copyright © 1971 by W W Norton & Company, Inc; lines from 'The Burning of Paper Instead of Children'. Copyright © 1993 by Adrienne Rich. Copyright © 1971 by W W Norton & Company, Inc from *Collected Early Poems: 1950–1970* by Adrienne Rich; and for e e cummings, 'in Just-' from *Complete Poems 1904–1962* by e e cummings, ed. George J Firmage. Copyright © 1991 by the Trustees for the e e cummings Trust and George James Firmage; Simon Ortiz for an extract from 'Passing Through Little Rock' published in Woven Stone, The University of Arizona Press (1992); Penguin UK and The Wylie Agency (UK) Ltd on behalf of the author for Allen Ginsberg, 'A Supermarket in California' and extracts from 'Howl' from *Allen Ginsberg, Collected Poems 1947–1980*, first published in *Howl and Other Poems*, 1956. Copyright © Allen Ginsberg 1954, 1984; Random House, Inc for extracts from Maya Angelou, 'On the Pulse of Morning'. Copyright © 1993 by Maya Angelou; Random House UK for Robert Frost, 'Fire and Ice', and with Henry Holt and Co for Robert Frost, 'Desert Places', 'The Secret Sits' and 'The Gift Outright' from *The Poetry of Robert Frost*, ed. Edward Connery Lathem. Copyright © 1936, 1942 by Robert Frost, © 1964, 1970 by Lesley Frost Ballantine, © 1969 by Henry Holt and Co, and with Harcourt, Inc for extracts from Sinclair Lewis, *Babbitt*, pp. 11–3, 203. Copyright © 1922 by Harcourt, Inc, renewed © 1950 by Sinclair Lewis; Rogers, Coleridge & White Ltd in association with International Creative Management, Inc on behalf of the author and Random House, Inc for extracts from E L Doctorow, *World's Fair*, pp. 232–3, 264. Copyright © 1985 by E L Doctorow; Sterling Lord Literistic, Inc on behalf of the authors for extracts from Amiri Baraka, 'Black Art' from *Black Magic Poetry*, City Lights. Copyright © 1969 by Amiri Baraka; and Anne Sexton, 'Sylvia's Death' from *The Complete Poems of Anne Sexton*, Houghton Mifflin Company. Copyright © 1981 by Anne Sexton; Viking Penguin, a division of Penguin Putnam Inc for an extract from Sherwood Anderson, 'Adventures' from *Winesburgh, Ohio* by Sherwood Anderson, intro. Malcolm Cowley. Copyright © 1919 by B W Huebsch; Copyright © 1947 by Eleanor Copenhaver Anderson; Yale University Press for extracts from Cathy Song, 'Lost Sister' from *Picture Bride* by Cathy Song (1983).

Every effort has been made to reach copyright holders; the publishers would like to hear from anyone whose rights they have unknowingly infringed.